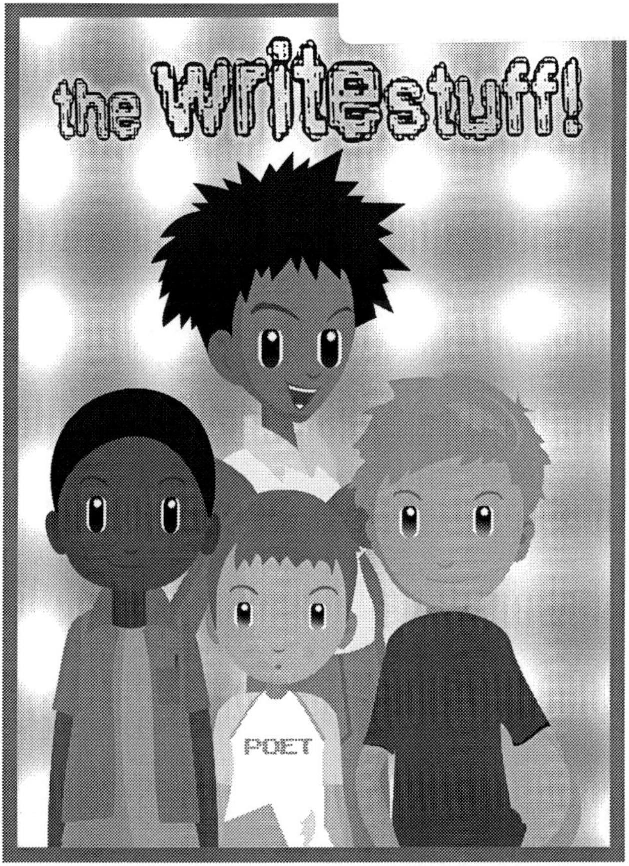
the Writestuff!
POET

Essex

Edited by Allison Dowse

First published in Great Britain in 2003 by
YOUNG WRITERS
Remus House,
Coltsfoot Drive,
Peterborough, PE2 9JX
Telephone (01733) 890066

All Rights Reserved

Copyright Contributors 2003

HB ISBN 0 75434 321 9
SB ISBN 0 75434 322 7

FOREWORD

This year, the Young Writers' The Write Stuff! competition proudly presents a showcase of the best poetic talent from over 40,000 up-and-coming writers nationwide.

Young Writers was established in 1991 and we are still successful, even in today's modern world, in promoting and encouraging the reading and writing of poetry.

The thought, effort, imagination and hard work put into each poem impressed us all, and once again, the task of selecting poems was a difficult one, but nevertheless, an enjoyable experience.

We hope you are as pleased as we are with the final selection and that you and your family continue to be entertained with *The Write Stuff! Essex* for many years to come.

CONTENTS

Hannah Underwood	1
Ketan Varma	1

Beauchamps High School

Holly Connors	2
Henry Field	2
Sophie Irwin	3
Amy Harding	4
Robert Stretch	4
Caroline Reading	5
Sam Lyon	6
Joshua Bull	6
Jessica Burrows	7
Charlie Morris	7
Amy Munday	8
Russell Colkett	8
Scott Hodges	9
Ben Hinton	10
Kimberley Osborne	10
Craig Howe	11
Victoria Dixon	11
Jordan Pearce	12
Rianne Bixby	13
Dan Ellis	13
Matthew Clark	13
Charlotte Adlem	14
William Taylor	15
Luke Rowe	16
Scott Rose	16
Melanie Johnson	17
Oliver Blunt	17
Zoe Chumbley	18
Ben Branscombe	18
Marc Maynard	19
Lisa Boswell	19
Jade Sackman	20

Tom Morl	20
Callum McCutcheon	21
Natalie Heath	21
Matt Hooper	22
Katie Mellia	22
Rebecca Turnbull	23
Simon Ellis	23
Stephen Fielding	24
Alex Hornsby	24
Jason Mortimer	25
Kirsty Farrant	25
Karen Bell	26
Kathryn Harrison	26
Ben Gotch	27
Claire Bagridge	27
Hayley Barrick	28
Scott Brindley	29
Lucy Miln	29
John Grantham	30
Jessica Richards	30
Demi Ward	31
Ryan Day	31
Leyla Manyera	32
Hollie Malster	32
Cyndi Stanton	33
Catherine Batt	33
Joe Olley	34
Jade Tussaud	34
Tom Jay	35
Lauren Brown	35
Kirsty Scorah	36
Sam Harris	36
Shayla Sloane	37
Andy Tilsley	37
Penelope de St Paër-Gotch	38
Katherine Murphy	39
Louis Steeves	40
Thomas Piggott	40

Carla Schooling	41
Lauren Day	41
Hayley Dunn	42
Amy Pepperell	42
Christopher Murphy	42
Demi Strong	43
Kerrie Longman	43
John Kirby	44
Zoe Batchelor	44
Brett Doherty	45
Thomas Hole	45
Kayleigh O'Sullivan	46
Laura Seeley	46
Charlotte Carroll	47
Stephen Munns	47

Brentwood School

Katie Dalby	48
Rebecca Freeman	48
Geet Chawla	49
Anjuli Valera	50
Sophie Bird	51
Emma Robertson	52
Rebecca Sentance	52
Charlotte Simpson	53
Belinda Boakye	53
Anna Rath	54
Katie Elias	54

Colchester High School

Ross King	55
Josh Rutledge	56
Ben De Luca	56
Nicholas Haydon	57
Tom Willis	58
Riyan Durrani	58
William Farrar	59
Benjamin Maytham	60

Robert Parkin	60
James Dodds	61
Matthew Chilvers	62
Kieran Stallard	62
Jonathan Gill	63
Louis Sargeant	64
Ben North	64
Adam Ross-Marrs	65
William Robertson	66
Alex Hutchings	66
Daniel Wright	67
Simon Alan Moorcroft	68
William Douglas	68
Dominic Brazington	69
Ashley Dawson	69
Thomas Biegel	70

Dagenham Priory Comprehensive School
Kayleigh Watson	71
Patience A Grugglsberg	72
Bill Ruel	72
Genevieve Smith	73

Friends' School
Charlotte Golding	74
Fergus Walsh	74
Camilla Oelman	75
Kenya Brading	76

Great Baddow High School
Christie Wright	77
Becky Breedon	78
Brendon Farrelly	78
Anna Manfredi	79
Sophie Cannon	79
Jade Woulfe	80
Louise Thomas	80
Paul Beard	81

Carys Kyei	81
Tommy Ecott	82
Daniel Filby	82
Camille Collinson	83
Jake Cochrane	83
Daniel Looney	84
Olivia Chitty	84
Holly Weeks	85
Samantha Knott	86
Victoria Roberts	86
Joe Collins	87
Stephen White	87
Daniel Bruce	88
Edward Rendell	88
Greg Flinders	89
Neil Searles	90
James Goddard	90
Shane Bone	91
Liberty Donald	91
Sam Haldane	92
James Hall	92
Jack Venn	93
Michael Regan	93
Ryan Baxter	94
Matt Skeoch	95
Adam Hone	95
Steven Riley	96

Hassenbrook GM School

James Edwards	96
Jonathan Shovlar	97
Eliott Farr	97
Chloe Flame	98
Daisy Flame	99
Victoria Sallows	100
Jade Gibbs	102
Karris Rowbotham	103
Hannah Southgate	104

Kayleigh North	104
Natasha Wareham	105
Aaron Gouge	106
Daniel Skinner	107
Natalie Godward	108
Joanna Pemberton	109
Shaun McIntosh	110
Adam Bulpitt	111
Vicky Abbott	112
Marie Sorenson	113
James Cummings	113
Matt Sandy	114
Charlotte Brainwood	114
Lettie Nice	115
Sophie Allison	116
Samantha Barnett	116
Hannah Shilling	117
Jack Conway	118
Ben Sullivan	119
Gary Shilling	120

Honywood School

Lisa Kemp	120
Charlotte Finch	121
Jean White	122
Rebecca Yexley	123
Matthew Roberts	124
Michael Howell	124
Jennifer Man	125
William Pearmain	126
Alex Whitelock	127
Jessica Barham	127
Lyall Horner	128
Jack Thomas	128
Rebecca Clarke	129
Emma Killick	129
Chloe Austin	130

Newport Free Grammar School
        Matt James Abbott   131
        Jodie Clay   132
        Deborah Hibbitt   132
        Nicole Younie   133
        Natalie Christie   134
        Natalie Howlett   135
        Simon Wilks   136
        Marshall Hulance   137
        Gemma Perman   138
        Eilidh Torbett   138
        Ben Williams   139
        Clare McPartland   140
        Helena Bland   140
        Laura Forman   141
        Felicity Fairweather   142
        Sarah Peak   142

Robert Clack Comprehensive Upper School
        Kayombo Chingonyi   143

Sir Charles Lucas Arts College, Colchester
        Candice H White   144

St Helena School, Colchester
        Jonathan Caumont   144
        Roxana Kashani   145
        Naomi Pike   146
        Alice Polley   146
        Emma Harrigan   147
        Verity Grimsey   148
        Sarah Halls   148
        Laura Price   149
        Amy Robinson   150
        Danielle Cheasley   151
        Ashleigh Martinez   151

South East Essex Sixth Form College
	Julianne Carter	152
	Lisa Winsor	153

The Plume School
	Michaela Dunn	153
	Tammy Wright	154
	Chris Herber	155
	Lianna Cudby	156
	Christopher Johnson	157
	Hanane Yahiaoui	158
	Charlotte Bacon	159
	Sophie Mardon	160
	Hayley Bond	161
	Alexandra Howat	162
	Sarah Wynn	163
	Daniel South	164
	Emma Pollard	165
	Tim Wade	166
	James Byrom	166
	Amy Baker	167

Thomas Lord Audley & Language College
	Daniel O'Sullivan	168
	Georgina Pacey	168
	Toni Peperell	169
	Amy Birch	170
	Mark Wynne	170
	Rachel Barnett	171
	Stacey Reubins	172
	Rebecca Emily Mary Readman	172
	Teshawna Fisher	173
	Lucy Beaumont	174
	Amanda Rand	174
	Peter Franklin	175
	Leighann Davison	175
	Steven Barrett	176
	Deanne MacDonald	176

Rebecca Wilson	177
Liam Bingle	177

Westcliff High School For Boys
Siôn Griffiths	178

Woodbridge High School
Shruti Kapoor	178
Rowena Knight	179

The Poems

PEOPLE

Why do people stand and stare?
Why look and glare?

Why do people not care?
Why are people so unfair?

Who is to blame
And what's their name?

This is not a funny game,
But there must be someone to blame.

Whose fault is all this?
Please give me a list.

What is the evidence to show
While the facts are low?

Which man in this row
And how do you know?

What will happen next?

Hannah Underwood

FULL MANY A MARVELLOUS SUNSET HAVE I SEEN

Full many a marvellous sunset have I seen,
Light red covering the sky,
The splendid sun performing alchemy on the world
Boiling fingernails slicing the world in two
Resplendent stars shining to Earth
Extraordinary colours filling the sky
The world is floating in the colourful sky
Huge fingernails letting the moon rise.
The moon playing it with the people.

Ketan Varma (11)

INSIDE A GIRL'S HEAD

Inside a girl's head it's pretty and pink.
Hearts and stars all around.
With hairbrush and make-up and
Perfume that take up
Most of the room to be found!

Inside a girl's head, gossip and jewellery
Necklaces, bracelets and rings,
Sashes and medals, trophies and photos
From beauty contests that she wins!

Inside a girl's head, make-up and fashion
Cute boys she tries to impress,
Handbags and jeans, trousers and belts
Stylish with her new Gucci dress!

Inside a girl's head, accessories and perfume,
Eye shadow, gloss and more,
Scrunchies and bobbles, hair grips and clips
Glittery nails galore!

Inside a girl's head, biscuits and chocolate
Juicy secrets she keeps,
She wipes off her make-up, gets into bed
For a girl has to have beauty sleep.

Holly Connors (12)
Beauchamps High School

I KNEW A MAN

I know a man who knew a man,
Who flew to the sun in a frying pan,
It got too hot and he could not settle
So he flew back home in a whistling kettle.

I know a man who knew a man,
Who flew to the moon in a watering can,
It got too cold living in an old crater,
So he flew back home in a cheese grater.

Henry Field (12)
Beauchamps High School

MY CHILDHOOD

From the very day
I came to this world
I was as happy as a fish in water
I was as happy as a newborn puppy
I had a smile that filled the room with light.

From the day I could walk
I took my first couple of steps
I was as slow as a tortoise
Trying to balance as though I was upon
A thin piece of rope like an acrobat.

But when it came to dinner time
I was like a monkey making a mess
Every time I had a yoghurt I tipped it over my head.

Bath time came in the evening
I splashed around like a duck having fun
Diving under the water like a mermaid.

The day had come to an end
It was time for bed
I went to sleep all cosy like a little puppy.

Sophie Irwin (11)
Beauchamps High School

THE BELL

As the bell rings,
you hear his chuckle flow through the sky
you smell a hint of peppermint
as it flows through the dark night.
The one sound he makes brings happiness
to all the children in school.
This is the sound of the bell.

The golden glow of the bell
shines through the village
and glows through the world.
His big chubby face smiles on the village
and spreads happiness to all.

The children stared eagerly at the bell
waiting for it to chime
But as the weeks went on
And the months went by
The bell gradually died.

Amy Harding (11)
Beauchamps High School

THE CRAB

The crab comes out of its shell.
In the morning it rings the bell.
The crab crawls lightly across the shiny sand
To listen to the nearby band.
It walks silently to the hut where the people shout
And the people jiggle about.
It finally arrives at its site
As the moon fades into the misty night.

Robert Stretch (11)
Beauchamps High School

MY PET PIG

My pet pig was the best in the world,
Her name was Rosie,
She was black as coal.

My pet pig was the sweetest thing ever,
Even if she was a little fat!
She was a pig after all!

My pet pig was just too heavy,
We had to carry her in a sheet,
Out to the van in which she was carried away.

I climbed in front
With my dad and brother,
The engine roared and off we went.

We stopped outside a big yard,
Goats were running round and round,
We lowered Rosie out the back.

We jumped back in,
And off we drove,
Leaving Rosie to die.

A few days later,
There was a phone call,
Rosie's dead! How could this happen?

I cried all day,
I cried all night,
I'll never sell my pets again.

Caroline Reading (11)
Beauchamps High School

BREAKFAST IN BED

Breakfast in bed
is a very good thing,
just think of the food
that they could bring.

Maybe some toast,
with some jam,
boiled egg
with rolled-up ham.

It's going to be tasty,
that's for sure,
once I've finished,
I'll ask for more.

Breakfast in bed,
is very good grub,
and it's definitely
food we all love!

Sam Lyon (11)
Beauchamps High School

WHAT AM I?

I never stop like an anthill
I belong on a face
I killed the dinosaurs
I made a mountain
I'm different all over the world
I'm measured in a clock
What am I?

Joshua Bull (11)
Beauchamps High School

THE COTTAGE

Down the lane,
Across the stream,
An acre-long forest stands tall.

Where bluebells grow,
And sparrows sing,
Down by an old brick wall.

Follow a trail of worn-down grass
Where foxes passed the night before.
Eyes are spying close to you.
Rats, foxes, mice and cats.

Your old home,
Your childhood memories,
Entangled in ivy,
You left so long ago.

Jessica Burrows (11)
Beauchamps High School

MY CLASS

This is a description of me and my class
Most of us come to school in a car.

Some of us are skinny
Some are small
Some are slim
And some are tall!

Sometimes we're good
Sometimes we're bad
Most of the time
The teacher goes mad!

Charlie Morris (11)
Beauchamps High School

WHY DO THEY CALL IT HOMEWORK?

Why do they call it homework?
It doesn't get done at home
It gets left in a corner
Or even a sauna
All burnt, or all alone.

If it's not at home it will be in the shed
All alone where the rats are dead
Not at home all neat on the table
Because I'll be downstairs watching cable

If it's not in the shed it will be in the bin
All yucky and crammed in a tin.
Those teachers are mad that say homework's a sin
Like
    I
      said
         it
           should
               be
                  in
                     the
                        bin!

Amy Munday (11)
Beauchamps High School

THE MAGIC DRAGON

The magic dragon swam many seas.
The magic dragon also had fleas
The magic dragon was sitting on a beach
eating a peach.
The magic dragon hit his head.
The magic dragon then went to bed.

He baked a cake
and slipped over his magic rake.
He went to the movies, he got a drink.
He went to the toilet and fell in the sink.
He saw the movie
and he thought it was groovy.

Russell Colkett (11)
Beauchamps High School

ICE CREAM POEM

The ice cream is just a soft, slushy cube of ice,
But somehow it tastes so very nice
But you have to eat it quick, otherwise
                            drip
                                 drip
                                      drip!

Your ice cream is *d*
                r
                 i
                  p
               p
                i
                 n
                  g
And you're trying to
Catch every drop
It's going all over your top
                        drop
                              drop
                                  drop!

Scott Hodges (11)
Beauchamps High School

YOU!

You!
Your head is like a computer, full of wonderful ideas.
You!
Your eyes are like marbles, shiny and clear.
You!
Your ears are like butterfly wings.
You!
Your lips are like a red, red rose.
You!
Your hands are like soft pillows.
You!
Your legs are soft and smooth like the bird on tele.

Ben Hinton (14)
Beauchamps High School

YOU!

You smell like old rotting flesh!
You look like something that crawled out of the bin
You sound like a man-eating monster
You move like a vampire in the night

You!

You smell like beautiful flowers
You look like you have beauty treatments every day
You sound heavenly 24 hours a day
You move like a butterfly in the wind

You are perfection!

Kimberley Osborne (11)
Beauchamps High School

You!

You!
Your eyes are like the midnight stars.
You!
Your smile is like the canyon sunset.
You!
Your laugh is like a Mozart piece.
You!
Your hair is like the Pacific waves.
You!
Your run is like a wild stag.
You!
Your hands are like the softest silk.
You!
Your arms are as soft as a baby's cheek.

Craig Howe (13)
Beauchamps High School

You!

You!
Your head is as hard as a rock
You!
Your face is as white as a ghost's
You!
Your ears are as small as a hamster's
You!
Your nose is wet like a puppy's
You!
Your lips are as small as a baby's
You!
Your belly is as big as a pig's.

Victoria Dixon (13)
Beauchamps High School

THE TORNADO

Rushing away from
the scene of the
crime. Anger and rage
take it over, pulling
and twisting metal
into distorted shapes.
Its fury comes from its
heart beating quicker
than a flash of
lightning. Not giving
any mercy to anyone in its
path. Destroying lives,
families and homes.
Ploughing through
the countryside
leaving its mark
everywhere it
goes.
You can
not tame it.
You can't
tame the
t
w
i
s
t
e
r!

Jordan Pearce (11)
Beauchamps High School

WHEN I WAS SMALL

When I was small
I was like a bouncy ball
My cheeks were as fat
As a hamster
When I was like a mole
I didn't want to look
Because I hated to read books.

Rianne Bixby (11)
Beauchamps High School

DARING MONKEY

As childish as a toddler
King of the jungle
Climbing, crazy, carefree
The monkey pelts me with its poo, my opponent
I grab my slingshot and shoot him with a stone.

Bang!

Dan Ellis (14)
Beauchamps High School

THE MOSQUITO

Humming like a well-tuned engine,
Marauder of the night,
Beastly, biting, buzzing brigand,
The mosquito bedevils me, my tormentor,
The humming, the humming . . .

Splat!

Matthew Clark (13)
Beauchamps High School

MY FAMILY

I know a woman who is loving and caring
    a woman who always understands me.
I know a woman who will always stand by me,
    this woman's my mum.

I know a man who is loving and kind,
    a man who's always willing to help.
I know a man who will always protect me,
    this man's my dad.

I know a boy who is funny and gentle,
    a boy who's always a friend to me.
I know a boy who will always be there for me,
    this boy's my brother.

I know a baby who is sweet and cute,
    a baby who's always there to make me laugh.
I know a baby who can stop my tears with one look,
    this baby's my brother.

I know a woman who is soft and gentle,
    a woman who's always there for me.
I know a woman who I can always rely on,
    this woman's my nan.

I know a man who is big and cuddly,
    a man who always has a way to make me laugh.
I know a man who I can always turn to,
    this man's my grandad.

I know a woman who is funny and caring,
    a woman who always knows what to say to make things better.
I know a woman who will always help me,
    this woman's my gran.

I know a man who is gentle and kind,
   a man who is always able to make anyone laugh.
I know a man who is always smiling,
   this man's my grandad.

I know a woman who I can always talk to,
   a woman who will always be there to listen to me.
I know a woman who I will always be close to.
   this woman's my great gran.

I know a man who is funny and weird,
   a man who is very intelligent.
I know a man who is always up for a challenge,
   this man's my uncle.

I know a woman who is pretty and bright,
   a woman who is like a big sister to me.
I know a woman who is a lot like me,
   this woman's my auntie.

I know a group of people who mean the world to me,
   a group of people who are always there for me,
I know a group of people who will always protect me,
   these people are my family.

Charlotte Adlem (12)
Beauchamps High School

FIRE

F   lickering through the burning house,
I   nnocent lives are taken.
R   oaring and raging,
E   ating anything in sight.

William Taylor (12)
Beauchamps High School

YOU!

You!
Your head is like a big rock
You!
Your eyes are like balls of ice
You!
Your ears are like an oven to melt blocks of ice
You!
Your insides of your nostrils are like a jungle
You!
Your mouth is like a tunnel
You!
Your hands are like ice packs
You!
Your belly is like a hippopotamus
You!
Your legs are like wobbly jelly
You!
Your backside is like an elephant.

Luke Rowe (13)
Beauchamps High School

COP STARS

Some are fat, some are slim
Some just never-workers, doughnut-eaters
Some just never get exercise
But one thing they're good at
Sorting out is pestercise,
Some are pop stars who can't sing
But I think we only have one word
Which is *Cop stars!*

Scott Rose (11)
Beauchamps High School

You!

You!
Your face is as fresh as a summer rose.
You!
Your eyes are like big balls of sunshine.
You!
Your skin is as soft as a kitten's fur.
You!
Your hair is as long as a mile.
You!
Your mouth is like a metal junkyard.
You!
Your hands are always as cold as ice.
You!
Your belly is as big as Great Britain.
You!
Your legs are like matchsticks.
You!
Your bottom is like a pair of massive hills.
You!

Melanie Johnson (13)
Beauchamps High School

My Cousin's Car

My Cousin Dan can drive really far
But only because he has a ZR
He goes really fast
But not on the grass
It's fun to race
And it has its pace
My cousin's car goes really far.

Oliver Blunt (11)
Beauchamps High School

YOU!

You!
Your head is like a bowling ball
You!
Your eyes are like white ping-pong balls
You!
Your ears are so big they're almost as big as Dumbo's
You!
Your mouth is like a pair of bent sausages
You!
Your hands are like a pound of meat
You!
Your belly is as big as a hamster's belly
You!
Your legs are like two baseball bats
You!
Your backside is like two big basketballs.
You!
Your tongue is like a big pink trampoline.

Zoe Chumbley (13)
Beauchamps High School

FAMILY

Families are here to stay. They never let you down.
Always here to say hello and to cheer you up
when you feel down.
Might even invite you around for a lovely dinner
I'm the luckiest of them all because my family
is the best in the world.
Love and care is what you get in a great family.
You can have a really good time if you have a No 1 family.

Ben Branscombe (11)
Beauchamps High School

You!

You!
Your eyes are like balls of fire
You!
Your ears are as big as your head
You!
Your head is like a fat balloon
You!
Your fingers are like a bunch of sausages
You!
Your head is like a melon
You!
Your belly is as big as a suitcase
You!
Your backside is like a mountain
You!
Your teeth are as green as a tennis ball.

Marc Maynard (13)
Beauchamps High School

My Mummy

There is always someone I can count on,
a person who is like a star in the sky, watching over me,
she's like a queen on a throne who adores me.

She will always help me with my homework
or if I'm upset, she's a diamond ring
and I love her dearly.

>My mum is the best mum
>in the world.

Lisa Boswell (12)
Beauchamps High School

You!

You!
Your head is like an eggshell
You!
Your eyes are like the full moon
You!
Your ears are as big as an elephant's
You!
Your nostrils are like two holes
at a train station that trains go through
You!
Your mouth is like a rabbit hole
You!
Your hands are like big rocks
You!
Your belly is like a big drum
You!
Your legs are like cricket bats
You!
Your backside is like a mountaintop
You!
Your hair is like straw and hay.

Jade Sackman (13)
Beauchamps High School

Hawk, Hawk

As free as the wind
Sovereign of the sky
Soaring, skimming, sailing
The hawk watches over me,
My guardian angel.
How I wish to be as free as he.

Tom Morl (13)
Beauchamps High School

You!

You!
Your head is like a balloon
You!
Your eyes are like a snake's
You!
Your nostrils are the size of jumbo jets
You!
Your mouth is like barbed wire
You!
Your hands are like two hard rocks
You!
Your belly is like a bowl of jelly
You!
Your legs are like logs
You!
Your backside is like an orange.

Callum McCutcheon (13)
Beauchamps High School

My Nan

My nan, she owns a van,
She lives in Essex,
She's the Countess of Wessex,
She makes me laugh because she's daft
And she has lots of money
And she's very funny.
We went to Paris,
She met a lady called Claris.
She went to Venice
And she loves playing tennis.
That's my nanny!

Natalie Heath (11)
Beauchamps High School

THE UNLUCKY MAN

The unlucky man,
Got run down by a van,
Swept out to sea,
And stung by a bee,
Shot with a gun,
Up his great big bum,
To put the cherry on the cake,
He got whacked with a rake.

The unlucky man,
Fell into a dam,
Got pummelled by thugs,
Attacked by giant bugs,
Fell out of bed,
And it hit him on the head,
Fell out of a tree,
Right on *me!*

Matt Hooper (11)
Beauchamps High School

CHOCOLATE

Chocolate, chocolate, is so great,
Chocolate, chocolate, is my mate.
Oh chocolate, chocolate, I love you.
Oh chocolate, chocolate, yes I do.

Chocolate, chocolate is so fine,
Chocolate, chocolate, you are mine,
Galaxy, Mars, KitKat too,
Toffee Crisp, Maltesers, I love you!

Katie Mellia (11)
Beauchamps High School

THE COUNTRYSIDE

The tall trees that rustle with the wind,
The country stream trickling through the forest,
Birds singing a peaceful tune,
A farmer's crops growing well.

Insects chirping everywhere,
Leaves start falling to the ground,
The crunching of acorns,
A whistle of the wind.

Squirrels running up trees,
A fox scurrying away,
A mole mound hidden behind trees,
Only the natural sounds can be heard.

Rebecca Turnbull (11)
Beauchamps High School

THE WEIRD WITCHES

'Which witch is rich?'
said the wiggly, whirly witch,
as she watched the worm wiggle
around the wall.

'Which witch is wobby?'
said the wiggly, whirly witch,
as she watched a wombat kicking a football.

'Which witch is worst?'
said the wiggly, whirly witch,
as she watched the Wonder-Bra
whizzing around the hall?

Simon Ellis (11)
Beauchamps High School

THE GOLDEN SPRIT

As cold as ice
    As thick as steel
The sprit is coming
    It is going to strike

It's creeping in shadows
    It knows when to strike
The sprit is coming
    It is going to strike

It's as sly as a fox
    It strikes when least wanted
And leaves its mark forever

It's the golden sprit!

It's the golden sprit
It can destroy
It can strike

The golden sprit!

Stephen Fielding (11)
Beauchamps High School

FRIENDS
(In Memory Of Robert Pavelin, R I P)

Friends are there when you are feeling blue,
They can cheer you up,
They will always be there for you,
Even if they disappear,
Or they go somewhere else,
You know they will always be near.

Alex Hornsby (11)
Beauchamps High School

Pam

There lives a lady called Pam,
She is a complete sham.
She likes to eat doughnuts,
If she eats too much she goes nuts.

She works as a teacher,
She knows Mrs Beacher.
She thinks she knows it all,
But really she knows nothing at all.

She eats like a pig,
She likes figs,
She works in Year 6,
She marks with no ticks.

She is very posh,
Her brother is Josh.
She is very old,
Her hands are cold.

Jason Mortimer (11)
Beauchamps High School

Dolphins

Dolphins splash
and dolphins dive.
Dolphins swim
off to hide!

Dolphins play
and dolphins watch.
Dolphins swim
around the clock!

Kirsty Farrant (11)
Beauchamps High School

OWL ALONE

Isolated, intimidated by what is going on
Outside his world, wanting to be appreciated,
Wanting to extend, like a snail
Coming out of its shell.

Reserved until the darkness spreads,
Until his time comes,
When he can emerge from the hole
And bring all feelings to the surface.

It's here, the time to expand,
The time to abandon all emotions.
Letting everything go, to become free
To become king of the woods.

Karen Bell (13)
Beauchamps High School

I AM A BIRD

I am a bird, young and free,
I am a flower, look at me,
I am a leopard, strong and mighty,
I am a cat, landing lightly.
I'm on the vase of Ming,
I'm being most everything.

I am springtime, I am a time.
I am the seal who swims all day,
I am the pole on the day of May.

I am here for those of you, the world,
For you're the hand and glove,
For my name is *love*.

Kathryn Harrison (11)
Beauchamps High School

WHY?

Sparrow flitting to and fro,
In the darkness watch him go,
Flying high, flying low,
Flying freely, watch him go.

In the darkness, flying high,
Going round in the sky,
If he falls he would die,
Watch him fly.

Once he flew throughout the sky,
Flying low, flying high,
So why?
Why did he die?

Ben Gotch (13)
Beauchamps High School

THE MOUSE

Scooting across the landing,
racing to get home.
Tiny, weak and vulnerable.
Scrawny, grey and long.
Whizzing past the staircase
wanting to be gone.
Through the gigantic doorway,
stopping dead in its tracks
this slender little creature
is confronted with an evil cat.
Dodging, diving and dancing around
attempting to escape a
dreadful fate!

Claire Bagridge (13)
Beauchamps High School

MY LION

Just me and my fears,
We wait together,
We shake like a leaf,
As we hear the sound.

Cackling, laughing, it gets louder,
We try and hide,
But those eyes, those blood-red eyes,
They stare at us from far and near.

The horrible grin,
That hyena wears,
It grabs us by the throat,
Suffocates and strangles.

Snap!
We break free from its glare,
But it makes it stronger,
Gathering its gang, it gets closer and closer.

Then it comes,
My saviour,
Joins me and my fears,
Sticks by our sides.

The intimidators become the intimidated,
They flee and run,
To get away from the
Roar!

I wave goodbye to my fears,
Slowly, but surely, they disappear.

Independent at last,
I have made a new friend,
I call them 'my lion'.

Hayley Barrick (13)
Beauchamps High School

WOLF MAN

The sun is shining in the sky
In the sky a bird flies by
The wind is slight but the water is fast
I see a man run past,
His sweat goes into the ground.
I sit here until the black sky comes down
An owl comes into my sight
I don't know what has run past me
But maybe the runner is still running
I look up at the moon
And see a man on it fishing in the sea
And slowly my hands turn into hair
Then all my body turns to hair
I howl for a moment,
Now I'm a wolf again on my own.

Scott Brindley (11)
Beauchamps High School

IT'S CHRISTMAS EVE!

It's Christmas Eve, it's Christmas Eve,
I'm so excited, I'm so excited.
I'll leave a mince pie out, I'll leave a mince pie out
And some milk, and some milk.
I'll go to sleep now, I'll go to sleep now.
I'm in my bed, I'm in my bed,
I'll lay down my head, knowing tomorrow
    there will be a stocking . . . on . . . my . . .
                            b
                             e
                              d
                                zzzzz!

Lucy Miln (11)
Beauchamps High School

WHEN I STARTED BEAUCHAMPS

When I started at Beachamps School,
I didn't know where anything was,
I felt such a fool!
When going from class to class
there was pushing and shoving and
I thought I would never get past.
Queuing for dinner was such a chore
I thought if I don't have food soon
I will drop on the floor.
Now I'm getting to know the ropes,
I feel like I'm more able to cope,
Some lessons I like, some I don't,
my favourite is English with Mrs Jones
who hardly ever moans!
So different from my other school.
So much homework, you don't know what to do,
Still I suppose it has to be done
and I must admit *some* of it is a little fun.
Well, time to get some sleep,
ready for the coming week.

John Grantham (11)
Beauchamps High School

PLAYTIME

I love playtime, that's why I go to school.
I play with all my friends, Bob, Peter, Jane and Paul.
We swing on the monkey bars, sometimes all day.
We also play football, that's usually in May!

Jessica Richards (11)
Beauchamps High School

WHAT A BABY!

When I was one,
I set off up and down the house,
As fast as a rocket,
And then I would fall fast asleep,
Like a little dormouse,
And in my cosy coat.

Then the next day,
I would be as slow as a snail
And be as good as gold,
Nibbling away at my food.

I would have a bath,
And pretend that a shark was chasing me,
I would be scared like one of my rattling toys.

What a baby I was!

Demi Ward (11)
Beauchamps High School

THE SNAKE

They glide across the jungle's floor all day long.
Lying there looking proud and fierce.
They are as sneaky as a crocodile
The snake scuttles, sneakily, searching for
                scared unprotected victims.
They are the kings of the jungle's lower level.

The prey is trapped, no way out!
The prisoner rebels but he is too weak.
He loses, a blood-splattered body.
The snake takes a bite. *Crunch!*

Ryan Day (14)
Beauchamps High School

INSIDE THE...!

Inside the cat's bright eyes, the moon's bright shine.
Inside the moon's bright shine, the swishing tail.
Inside the swishing tail, the rusty autumn leaves.
Inside the rusty autumn leaves, the cat's fur.
Inside the cat's fur are the hues of mountain and heather.
Inside the hues of mountain and heather is the cat's prey,
                                the frightened little rabbits.
Inside the frightened little rabbits, the rabbits' tears.
Inside the rabbits' tears is the cat's bite.
Inside the cat's bite, the flow of blood.
Inside the flow of blood is the smell of success.
Inside the smell of success, the twitch of whiskers.
Inside the twitch of whiskers . . .
                The cat's bright eyes!

Leyla Manyera (11)
Beauchamps High School

FIRE

Fire, its orangy flames reach high in the sky,
burning continuously.
Its eyes transfixed to anything that dares come too close.
Ashes like fireflies light the area.
Wood burnt to ashes, lifeless forever.
Flames raging like anger gradually getting bigger to blazes,
Then into an outrageous inferno, then suddenly the fire stops.
But does it?
Secretly it carries on in the hearts of those who are worthy
                                of lighting it again.

Hollie Malster (11)
Beauchamps High School

CHARACTERISTIC CYNDI

When I was born I was as red as a ruby.

When I was a little child, my mum
thought I was very wild, like a hyena.

After that, when I grew up more, then
I could nearly reach the door like my dad.

Later on, I was getting older, then I was
growing as high as my mum's shoulder.

A few years on I was going to school
then I thought I was as cool as my friend.

After that I went to Beauchamps High, which
is really big, honestly, it's as tall as the sky.

Cyndi Stanton (11)
Beauchamps High School

ME, WHEN I WAS YOUNGER

When I was born I was as small as a bumblebee,
As light as a butterfly.
When I was younger I was as sleepy as a bear.
I was as bouncy as a spring,
As sweet as sugar.
I was like a ravenous cat, making noises like a bat.
Kangaroo Catherine, that was me, as mad and reckless
                                        as I could be.
When I slept I was as peaceful as a person in their grave.
Now I'm older, I act more my age.

Catherine Batt (11)
Beauchamps High School

ONLY FOOLS AND HORSES

O is for Only Fools and Horses
N is for Nelson Mandela House
L is for London
Y is for you know it makes sense

F is for full English breakfast
O is for on the booze
O is for ongoing deals
L is for late nights
S is for Sheeney

A is for Albert
N is for Nag's Head
D is for Del Boy

H is for Hookey Street
O is for owing money
R is for Raquel
S is for selling
E is for engagements
S is for stupid (Trigger).

Joe Olley (11)
Beauchamps High School

LILAC

L ilac is my favourite colour
I t's pale and soft.
L ove lilac very much
A nd blue is nice as well.
C olour of my room is lilac.

Jade Tussaud (12)
Beauchamps High School

CHILDHOOD DREAMS

I wanted to be a fireman,
I wanted a good job,
I wanted one hundred million quid,
And my name was *Bob!*

As crazy as a nuthouse,
I ran around my home,
As fast as a cheetah,
Not as quiet as a gnome!

The speed I went was fantastic,
Speeding like a rocket,
But as I went round a corner,
I ran into a socket!

Zzzzzzzzzzzzzzzzz!

And that was the end of *Bob!*

Tom Jay (11)
Beauchamps High School

BEAUCHAMPS

Beautiful fields,
Excellent education,
Awarded for excellence,
Understanding children,
Caring teachers,
Hard-working,
Aiming for the top,
Making progress,
Performing well,
Successful school.

Lauren Brown (12)
Beauchamps High School

GLORIOUS SEASONS!

Winter's snowflakes daintily fall,
Her icicles forming with a shiny smile,
With mince pie, milk and carrots waiting,
She's loving and giving all around.

Spring's newborn birds flying
Newly-born lambs dancing with her,
Upon the sweet grass daisies grow,
Joy all around.

Her heat is rising for summer,
She cheekily makes ice cream melt,
With ice cubes forming,
Happiness and cheekiness all around.

Autumn's tears are drifting down,
Orange, red and green,
She's beautiful but sad inside,
She is a total dream.

Kirsty Scorah (11)
Beauchamps High School

CHRIS

There is a man called Chris and he is a lorry driver.
He's such a mad driver
He only gets a fiver
He's such a nutter
He drives past cars at 100mph
If he goes any faster his lorry will be on fire
He screeches through London as fast as he can
He will probably get a six-month ban!

Sam Harris (11)
Beauchamps High School

NIGHT-TIME OWL

The clock strikes twelve
The world continues with its stillness of sleeping
But outside, in the coldness of wicked winter
Something stirs

Eyes, suddenly open wide
The head twitches
Wings stretch like sleepy children's arms
And it looks and it listens in the silent moonlight.

Then there's a noise
A rustle, a scuttle, a field mouse
Concentrating eyes peer into the darkness
Swoop!
Tonight's meal is caught and ready

All too soon day starts to raise its head
The world awakens, but that something doesn't
That something snuggles in a tree
And tired eyes begin to fall

The owl!

Shayla Sloane (13)
Beauchamps High School

ANDY'S LIFE

When I was one I was as small as a pebble
When I was two I was like a little rebel
When I was three I was like a dog eating his food
When I was four I was like a whoopee cushion
When I was five I was as stealthy as a tiger
When I was six I was as fast as a rabbit
When I was seven I was like an angel from Heaven, not.

Andy Tilsley (11)
Beauchamps High School

SOMEWHERE IN TIME

Somewhere in time there is a place,
Where war and suffering rip the land.
Somewhere in time there is a place,
Where diseases flourish and sorrows reign.
Somewhere in time there is a place,
Where happiness and health shrivel and die.
Somewhere in time there is a place,
Where tears make rivers and pain stays always.
Is it in the past or happening now?
You decide.

Somewhere in time there is a place,
Where peace and goodwill fix all holes.
Somewhere in time there is a place,
Where health flourishes and happiness reigns.
Somewhere in time there is a place,
Where diseases catch themselves and die.
Somewhere in time there is a place,
Where sorrows catch fire and burn to death.
Somewhere in time there is a place,
Where tears of laughter fall like rain.
Somewhere in time there is a place,
Where joy is permanent emotion.
Is it the present or still to come?
You decide.

Somewhere in time there is a place,
Where good and evil are in the balance.
Somewhere in time there is a place,
Where sorrow and joy are alternate emotions.

Somewhere in time there is a place,
Where health sometimes gives way to illness.
Somewhere in time there is a place,
Where tears and laughter take their turns.
Is it the past, now or yet to come?
You decide.

Penelope de St Paër-Gotch (11)
Beauchamps High School

TEXT FACES

:-)	Smiling face is happy
:-(	Unhappy face is sad
:'-(	This poor face is tearful
:-D	But that one is quite glad
:-0	That one there is shocked
:-/	And this one isn't sure!
;-)	There's a face that's winking
1-0	But that one's rather bored
<:- 1	That face feels quite stupid
:-X	This says, 'my lips are sealed'
0:-)	This is quite an angel
:-~)	But this one has a cold

Whatever you feel like,
Whether it's happy, bored or glad,
Let them all be good things,
And none of them be bad!

Katherine Murphy (11)
Beauchamps High School

MY CHILDHOOD

I wished I was Superman,
I wished I had a job,
but at the end of it all,
I had to stick with being a dog.

I was as mad as a monkey,
as crazy as a bee,
but when it was time to go home,
I would scream and wee.

I wanted to be an astronaut,
and get good pay,
but all-in-all,
I would rather play all day.

Louis Steeves (11)
Beauchamps High School

FOOTBALL THEME

I play for a football team,
I always know a theme,
I'm out there on the right,
Sometimes in the spotlight,
My mate plays defence,
Sometimes his offence,
My team's Trinity,
We've scored infinity,
I shout at the team,
'This is my theme.'

Thomas Piggott (11)
Beauchamps High School

WHEN I WAS LITTLE

When I was little I was as cute as a baby kitten,
especially when I put on my mittens,
I was born in the winter,
and cried when I had my first splinter

My mouth was a big as a lion yawning,
early in the morning
and I cried as loud as a tiger roaring.

Now I'm sitting in English class,
listening to my work task,
suddenly I go *pop!* Like a firework
and I feel a total jerk.

Carla Schooling (11)
Beauchamps High School

UNTITLED

When I was little I was
as cute as a cat,
My family took a picture of me
in my pink bobble hat,
I cried in the morning
like a tiger roaring.

I was born in the spring
and I liked to sing.

Up flew my top
as Carla went pop!

Lauren Day (11)
Beauchamps High School

BEAUCHAMPS

B is for *Beauchamps,* the best school in the world
E is for *English,* we'd better learn to spell
A is for *apparatus* that we use in the gym
U is for *up* the stairs, put your walking boots on
C is for *computers* that always seem to crash
H is for *history,* where the old Romans live
A is for *art,* we will get messy
M is for *music,* you are out of tune
P is for *physical education,* phew, that was tiring!
S is for *study,* which is why we go to Beauchamps.

Hayley Dunn (11)
Beauchamps High School

MY BEAUCHAMPS POEM

B is for *best,* the best school here.
E is for *enemies,* there are none.
A is for *anger,* only in the teachers.
U is for *us,* we are one.
C is for *competition,* we will try to win.
H is for *history.*
A is for *agreement.*
M is for *memorable* moments.
P is for *plays,* we love them.
S is for *support,* we have lots of support.

Amy Pepperell (11)
Beauchamps High School

A PRECIOUS LOSS

Scuttling along, silently, looked upon, not interesting
Engulfed among a sea of people.
Day after day after day
A bottomless pit of fear, sorrow, deprivation.

Wave upon wave splashing upon it
No way out, nowhere to go
Jailed, doomed to eternal loneliness.
One person wishing he could see it,
                          find a way in.

Christopher Murphy (13)
Beauchamps High School

SWEETS

S   weets, sweets, everyone loves sweets
W here, where can I find sweets?
     What shall I do? I have no sweets.
E   at, eat, I'll eat lots of sweets,
     make myself fat.
E   ver, forever, me and sweets,
     I'll eat, I'll eat until I drop.
Together, together, me and sweets
     we'll be together forever.
S   weets, sweets, everyone loves sweets.

Demi Strong (11)
Beauchamps High School

MY HAMSTER, SILKEY

H e sleeps sound nearly all day long
A mazingly he flips off the walls
M issing him every time I go out
S ilkey crawls about like a lost toddler
T iny and grey is what he looks like
E ating all the time, soon he will burst
R emembering the day I got him makes me
                                  smile!

Kerrie Longman (11)
Beauchamps High School

SPORT

S coring a goal against Greece from David Beckham took England to the World Cup 2002.

P assing is important in any sport because it can lead to a goal.

O ffside means if the ball is played after the defender it is offside.

R acing horses is very popular and lots of people bet money on them.

T alk to your teammates and shout if you want the ball.

John Kirby (11)
Beauchamps High School

TREASURED MOMENTS

When I was born I howled like a wolf,
Or maybe it was more like a dog.
When I was one I was as loud as an elephant,
Or maybe I was as quiet as a mouse.
When I was two, I was like a jack-in-a-box,
Or maybe like a china doll.
When I was three I liked to sit on my dad's knee,
Or maybe I liked to sit on my own.
When I was four, I wanted to grow up,
Or maybe not.

I am like a set of scales.

Zoe Batchelor (11)
Beauchamps High School

THE SIMPSONS

T he Simpsons is one of my favourite programmes on TV.
H omer is the dad of Bart, Lisa and Maggie.
E vil Mr Burns is the millionaire of Springfield.

S pringfield is where the Simpsons live.
I t is on every night on Sky One.
M aggie is the youngest Simpson.
P ictures are drawn by Matt Groening.
S pringfield Elementary is where the children go.
O n Sundays they go to church.
N ext door live the Flanders.
S eymor Skinner is in charge of the school.

Brett Doherty (11)
Beauchamps High School

THE SNOW

The glitter,
The shine,
It's all around us everywhere,
So it's Christmas time and everyone joins in,
And the fun is here.

Let's join hands and sing the Christmas carol,
As glittery as the stars,
As bright as the sun,
It's the snow
And it's all around us everywhere.

Thomas Hole (11)
Beauchamps High School

The Football Match

The football match began:
Moaning and groaning like a bunch of kids.
Hissing and kissing,
And arguing and targeting.

And hitting and spilling,
And clapping and slapping,
And rattling and battling,
And fighting and biting,
And jumping and bumping,
And running and humming,
And singing and pinging,
And kicking and nicking,
And then there's a . . .
    Goal!

Kayleigh O'Sullivan (11)
Beauchamps High School

EastEnders

E verybody likes this,
A sleep some people may be,
S taring at me all night long,
T V, that's me, that's me!
E ven though some people can see,
N ever
D are to turn me off!
E astEnders, EastEnders are the best
R eminder not to turn me off!

Laura Seeley (11)
Beauchamps High School

LIFE IS ...

Life is a kaleidoscope,
From one perspective, chaos
From another, perfect symmetry.

Life is a curious animal,
Inquisitive play,
Concludes in knowledge.

Life is a bag of pick 'n' mix,
You never can predict
What will derive.

Life is a burning flame,
It may grow, change,
For better, for worse.

Life is a new morning air,
You cannot prepare,
For what you cannot see.

Life is a baby,
Newborn, new ideas,
A new life.

Charlotte Carroll (14)
Beauchamps High School

FISH

Fish, fish, are so pretty,
Some are colourful like a goldfish
And some are ugly like a guppy.
I like fish because they are so colourful.

Stephen Munns (11)
Beauchamps High School

AUTUMN

Mist in the morning,
Ochre leaves falling
From the trees,
The weeping willow,
Hanging down,
Wilting plants, grass going brown.

Conkers and chestnuts,
Crocuses and lavender,
Ivy changing red,
Rosebuds in the rose garden,
Lichen, dying or dead.

Lifeless, quiet, algae on the pond.
Apples falling from the trees,
Rotting apples,
Moss on the ground.

Bees on the flowers,
Ducks on the pond, evergreen trees,
Red berries ripening,
Hoverflies nearby,
The days getting shorter,
Autumn is beginning.

Katie Dalby (11)
Brentwood School

AUTUMN

Mist rises in the morning.
The wind is swirling,
Children playing conker fights,
Hands are cold,
The sun is hiding behind the clouds,
The leaves make a crunch if you step on them,
Squirrels hide their nuts and acorns in trees,

The bees try hard to make honey,
Leaves changing to reds, yellows, golden browns,
The days are shorter,
The clocks go back,
Christmas is coming
So get out your sack!

Rebecca Freeman (11)
Brentwood School

AUTUMN

The white mist-covered, pale blue sky;
complements the haziness of the lazy sun.
The chilly, frost-bitten airy breeze,
tears the warmth, stinging the cheeks.

One by one, a bronze maple leaf falls;
coiling, crisping, crunched by the step.
The glittering dew on erect blades of grass,
spoilt by the touch of the gold-rimmed leaves.

The aged auburn apples hang loosely in clumps,
looking proud over their rotted friends.
Immaculate, glistening spider webs whole;
long-legged insects ripping their frail print.

The last of the eye-catching bloomed flowers;
the birth of the glossy red berries.
Goodbye to the sweet rosy smells of summer,
Good morning to the fiery shower of burnt colour.

Geet Chawla (14)
Brentwood School

AUTUMN

Summer is over, autumn is here,
The sweet little buzz of a bee in my ear,
The song of the birds flying swiftly above,
The peaceful blue sky with the beautiful white doves.

The rustle of leaves as they fall crisp to the floor,
One, two and many more,
The sweet aroma of the late-blooming flowers,
The apples and pears falling with a thud at all hours.

The variations of colour, red, yellow, brown,
All lying on the floor like a beautiful leaf gown,
The dew lying fresh on a spider's web,
With cats watching the last piece of sun on their leafy bed.

Oh, the misty rays of the sun at its last,
The auburn, gold, bronze colours coming through very fast,
The breeze blowing the withered leaves off the soon-bare trees,
The calm water with the occasional ripple at ease.

Hats and scarves coming out very soon,
Shadows against the wall at noon,
The ice covering the grass
Like a transparent blanket
Summer is over
And autumn
Is here.

Anjuli Valera (13)
Brentwood School

AUTUMN

The hot days of summer are
coming to an end,
and the cold days of autumn are
arriving again.
Red, yellow, gold and brown,
the colours of the crunchy leaves.
Spiders weaving cobwebs white.
Birds singing in the tall bare trees.
A soft breeze, a sway of a tree
as the wispy clouds fill the sky.
The last flowers blossom.
The last flowers wilt.
Children wrapped up in coats and scarves
crashing through the crispy leaves.
A drop of rain falls down from the sky
landing in the grass, laden with dew.
The wind is blowing and the rain
is falling,
Autumn is ending, winter is
arriving.
It went so fast we'll have
to wait,
till this time
next year, it
will be
back
again.

Sophie Bird (13)
Brentwood School

AUTUMN

Birds singing in the bare
brown trees,
the crisp fresh morning air,
that cold and bitter, blowy light breeze,
that blows right through my hair.

The green grass with the morning dew,
the lovely bright blue sky,
the lavender that's come through new,
which people walk on by.

The flowers which are really nice,
the crunchy leaves on the ground.
For everything there is no price,
for this paradise I have found.

Emma Robertson (13)
Brentwood School

AUTUMN

The autumn leaves are changing colour,
From green to golden, red and brown,
I watch them gently fall from trees,
And lie upon the grassy ground.

The conkers fall from high above
As a squirrel scampers to its drey,
To hide from the coming winter season,
Above the sky is turning grey.

The animals are going to sleep,
The birds fly to a warmer place,
Everyone now knows that it is autumn.
The cold mist presses on my face.

Rebecca Sentance (11)
Brentwood School

AUTUMN

The acorns are falling to the ground.
Under the trees apples are found.
The trees are shedding their golden leaves.
Umbrellas are blowing inside out in the breeze.

It gets dark at four.
There is no sun anymore.
The clouds are covering most of the sky.
Now summer is gone, the sun has come to die.

The big chestnut trees
Are covered with many leaves.
They are golden and brown
And one by one they flutter down.

Charlotte Simpson (11)
Brentwood School

HER SONG

In me it will forever play,
Submerge me in its woeful tune,
Or lift the spirits of the day,
Where memories unyielding loom,
Tomorrow's fearful drums do beat,
A merciless overwhelming drone,
Vulnerable in a crowd I wait,
Straining for her calm sub-tone.
For now hark back to safer times
Secure and warm in her caress.
Rocking gently to lullabies.
Without question I see unrest;
But now too late, and then too long.
All unremaining but her song.

Belinda Boakye (17)
Brentwood School

SATURDAY MORNING SCHOOL

I'm getting quite tired by Saturday morning,
a sixth day of make-up and dangerous high heels.
My charade is thinning and I can't help yawning,
the laughter and smiling is starting to peel.

His jokes no longer amuse me
I don't care that her goldfish is dead
I'm getting quite sick of pretending to be
this girl who is everyone's friend.

Pretending to work, pretending to smile,
pretending I'm not really smoking,
pretending that I don't need to cry
on Saturday - you must be joking!

But the truth of the matter, I don't really care,
just as long as I, don't fall down the stairs!

Anna Rath (17)
Brentwood School

AUTUMN

Scarlet and white speckled with pink are geraniums,
Fruit grows and falls off trees,
Gold, red, orange and brown are the colour of old leaves,
Crunch, crunch, as I walk through the leaves on the ground.

Birds have flown and left their nests,
Bright red roses smell lovely,
Whereas the angel trumpets only last a day,
Downy, browny baby ducks are getting older.

Weeping willows hang over a pond,
Fig leaves shaped like hands,
Berries and spiked leaves on holly trees,
Autumn is here and it is getting cold.

Katie Elias (11)
Brentwood School

ME!

Me!
My feet are like blocks of cheese,
Me!
My toes are like little peas,
Me!
My knees are like cricket balls,
Me!
My thighs are like apple pies,
Me!
My stomach is like a piece of haddock,
Me!
My chest is as hard as a treasure chest,
Me!
My head is like an Easter egg,
Me!
My eyes are blue like the sea,
Me!
My nose is like a jacket button,
Me!
My lips are like candyfloss,
Me!
My ears are like cherry drops.

Me! I'm Ross King.

Ross King (11)
Colchester High School

ME!

Me!
My face is round like a ball
Me!
My tummy is like a bucket
Me!
My fingers are like chopsticks
Me!
My feet are like rocks
Me!
My mouth is like a black hole
Me!
My hair is like a fluffy cat
Me!
My eyes are like the moon at night
Me!
My knees are like bricks
Me!
My chest is hairy like a racoon
Me!
My hands are like wings
Me!

Josh Rutledge (11)
Colchester High School

ME!

Me!
My eyes are as blue as the sky
Me!
My hair is as brown as an autumn leaf
Me!
My laugh is as cackly as a witch
Me!
My thoughts are as cheeky as a chimp

Me!
My nose is as round as a dome
Me!
My lips are as green as a blade of grass
Me!
I am as wild as the sea
Me!

Ben De Luca (11)
Colchester High School

M<small>E</small>!

Me!
My hair is like a thorn bush
Me!
My head is like a boulder
Me!
My fingers are like shrivelled worms
Me!
My eyes are like glass marbles
Me!
My neck is like a lamp post
Me!
My chest is hairy like an ape
Me!
My ears are like radar dishes
Me!
My teeth are like burned tree stumps
Me!
My nose is like a rotten carrot
Me!
My smell is like a compost heap

   Revolting!

Nicholas Haydon (11)
Colchester High School

Me!

Me!
My head is like an ostrich egg.
Me!
I have eyes that shine like the sun.
Me!
I have hair like a thorn bush.
Me!
I have teeth as black as coal.
Me!
I have a nose like a light bulb.
Me!
I have feet as big as flippers.
Me!
I have legs as long as fence panels.
Me!
I have arms as long as a javelin's.
Me!

Tom Willis (11)
Colchester High School

Me!

Me!
My eyes are bloodshot-red like the pits of Hell.
Me!
My head has horns sticking out as sharp as a bull's horns.
Me
My hair is as black as can be.
Me!
My body's big and muscular like Mr Olympia.

Me!
I have a tail with a point coming out of my rear.
Me!
I'm always holding onto a pitchfork like a baby attached to its mother.
Me!
It's funny because I'm exactly like the Devil.
Me!
Oh wait, that is me, *the Devil!*

Riyan Durrani (11)
Colchester High School

ME!

Me!
My teeth are like rocks.
Me!
My hair is like a mop.
Me!
My legs are like sticks.
Me!
My belly is like a rugby ball.
Me!
My ears are like someone's bad breath.
Me!
My hands are like wine bottles.
Me!
My neck is like a radiator.
Me!
My glasses are like the bottom of bottles.
Me!

William Farrar (11)
Colchester High School

Me!

Me!
My teeth look like white, clean paper.
Me!
My head looks like an apple.
Me!
My ears look like an elf's ears.
Me!
My nostrils look like a black hole.
Me!
My legs look like a mountaintop.
Me!
My eyes flare like a roaring fire.
Me!
My teeth chatter like ice.
Me!

Just . . . me!

Benjamin Maytham (11)
Colchester High School

Me!

Me!
My nose is like a vacuum cleaner.
Me!
My teeth are as green as grass.
Me!
My eyes are as red as a flame.
Me!
My hair is like a haystack.

Me!
My face is like a gargoyle.
Me!
My cheeks are like two balloons.
Me!
My arms are like two chair legs.
Me!
My feet smell like mouldy cheese.

Robert Parkin (12)
Colchester High School

ME!

Me!
My hair is like a hedgehog's
Me!
My nose is like a blob
Me!
My eyes are like slits in a mask
Me!
My mouth is like a postbox
Me!
My hands are like a teddy bear's
Me!
My toes smell like rotten cabbage
Me!
My nails are like pieces of bark
Me!
My head is like a dustbin.

James Dodds (12)
Colchester High School

THE SNAKE

I hear rustling,
Rustling in the grass
Everyone on guard
For there's a snake in the yard
Mum's going mad
Dad's going spare
But it's all too late
Out it strikes
Black as death
Long as tape
Side-winding across the grass towards the house
Hissing and spitting
Deadly or not, nobody knows
Small, long, not even inches tall
But
So deadly, venomous and ready to attack
After a while the snake goes away
Like a terrorist
To appear again in the worst way possible.

Matthew Chilvers (12)
Colchester High School

THE SNAKE

The stealthy snake slithered along
Stalking its victim in the noonday heat
The piercing eyes, its blood-red skin
Hissing meanly to itself

Its menacing head swaying from side to side
Licking its lips with its black forked tongue
Its deadly spit, its killing jaw
Moving subtly along

Its victim stood before it, totally unaware
And in a flash with a fatal bite
The victim was dead, the deed was done
And the snake had gone.

Kieran Stallard (12)
Colchester High School

ME!

Me!
My head is like a television
Me!
My eyes are like the dials
Me!
My ears are like the aerials
The room lights up when I smile!

Me!
My mouth is like the speaker
Me!
My legs are like the stand
Me!
My arms are like wires
I am very grand

Me!
My feet are like remote controls
Me!
My stomach is like the screen
Me!
My nose is like the volume button
I'm the strangest TV you've ever seen!

Jonathan Gill (11)
Colchester High School

THE DRAGON

His wings spread out and started flapping,
Like a bird about to take-off,
His very large figure towered over me,
Casting a great big shadow,
His large webbed feet stood strong on the ground,
His skin was rough and bumpy,
It had a sort of sliminess,
His eyes bulged out,
His body was a very bright red like a fire's flame,
He was about as tall as a giant,
On each of his scaly feet were five long and pointed claws,
As shiny as ivory tusks,
The long tail swayed back and forth,
The tail was an arrow, long and pointed,
The fierce eye on the end of his tail watched me intently,
Clouds of smoke started coming from his nostrils,
Like a volcano about to erupt,
Then out came the lava,
Burning everything in its way.

Louis Sargeant (12)
Colchester High School

THE GREEN MAMBA SNAKE

The fluorescent green skin,
Glinting in the sun,
Moving in the long green grass
Hissing bitterly
As it side-winds silently along

On alert
As it scuttles on the dry dirt
Making a twisting and twirling sound,
Hunting on unaware prey,
Cruelly curling as it gets ready to attack

It strikes on a minute mouse,
A last high-pitched squeak
Before the vicious venom takes effect,
The snake waits for it to stop writhing,
Then swallows it whole
And disappears into the vast jungle.

Ben North (12)
Colchester High School

HUNTING

The snake stealthily stalks its luckless prey
Sliding through the sand,
Rippling through the reeds
And menacing in the mud.

Its malicious gaze as cold as ice
Its emerald scales glinting in the sun,
Its muscular coils as strong as iron,
Its poison as deadly as the hunter's gun.

Winding over the savannah
Over the deserted grasslands
Its senses as sharp as a knife
It smells, it sees a disturbance in the reeds.

It writhes into the mud
Moves in for the kill and strikes!
Fangs out, tongue flicks,
Fur flies, body strains . . . silence!

The poison does its deadly work
The body falls limp
As the rat's eyes see last light
The snake moves out into the evening breeze.

Adam Ross-Marrs (12)
Colchester High School

Mytho

When I looked at Mytho,
I saw a body like a snake's,
two strong claws
and a horn
that looked like a bolt of lightning.
He had chains bedraggled
across his long and winding body.
Never before had I seen
such an imposing figure.
His body was the colour of a clear sky.
His hair, grey, which gave the effect
of a wise creature,
flowing in the wind.
His wings, jagged, were like snow
on a winter's morning,
without a speck of dirt on them.
Such a peaceful creature
soaring through the air like a dove . . .

William Robertson (11)
Colchester High School

The Snake

It's a snake, it's a snake.
Look at its jet-black and ruby-red
scaly skin slithering across the grass.
Its back, its back, with its fangs
as white as snow.
Look, look, it's a mouse, snap!
The snake swallows it whole.

Yes, yes, it's going, it's going,
slithering along quietly,
scuttling its slink slender body
behind it, hissing with its tongue.
Quick, quick, run, run,
before it comes again.
I can hear its violent hiss, and
the thought of that liquorice tongue!

Alex Hutchings (12)
Colchester High School

BEAST

I stood frozen to the spot
it had eyes like saucers.
They were as large as pork pies
and stared straight at me.
Its skin was shiny and rough,
green in colour with large lumps
here and there.
It stood on its back legs,
rearing up at me.
It gave me the impression
of an ugly beast.
I would not like to meet it
on a dark night in an alley.
It's a good job I'm looking
at a monster in a book -
I've only imagined
just a little bit more!

Daniel Wright (12)
Colchester High School

THE SNAKE

The forest-green snake slithered sneakily
through the dry, dusty earth, its body wriggling
dangerously through the piercing heat.

The blood-red snake slithered bitterly along
the green lush ground, hissing violently,
sneaking up on its unsuspecting prey,
waiting to pounce.

The jet-black snake, slimy, scaly, streaked
through the long grass, silently, innocently
waiting, waiting, waiting for something
innocent to come into view.

The multicoloured snake, curling, slithering
unnoticed in its glass home in a corner of a
room, waiting, wondering, when I shall be free,
free from this glass prison?

Simon Alan Moorcroft (13)
Colchester High School

THE SNAKE

The shiny snake scuttles along the sparkling sand,
Its scaly, slippery skin and its vivid orange splashes,
Will kill any small mammals in its path.

The serpent side-winds slowly through the grassy surroundings,
Passing other insects on its way,
Silent as the wind, it slithers and glides along.

Then camouflaged behind a fallen tree,
Patiently waiting, watching, while listening, then pouncing.
It attacks and cracks the skull of its prey.

William Douglas (12)
Colchester High School

THE SNAKE AND THE VOLE

The slimy-green snake slithers from the blazing sunlight
Under a cool boulder and out of sight.
It is sleeping but constantly aware
Of vibrations and slight movements in front of its sleepless stare.

A scuttling vibration of a vole alerts it to its senses.
Its head goes up and body tenses.

As the sun shines on its scaly skin, as the grass is scoured,
A quick jerk of his head and the vole is devoured.

Stalked until death.

Dominic Brazington (12)
Colchester High School

ME!

Me!
My eyes are like fires.
Me!
My hair is like an untamed forest.
Me!
My smile is like the sun.
Me!
My hands are like hammers.
Me!
My legs are as strong as steel.
Me!
My body is like a barrel.
Me!
My back is as steep as a mountain.

Ashley Dawson (12)
Colchester High School

ME!

Me!
My eyes are brown like bark,
Me!
My nose is like moulded putty,
Me!
My mouth is pale like the moon,
Me!
My hair is brown like dead grass,
Me!
My face changes colour with the weather like a chameleon,
Me!
My arms are like tubing,
Me!
My fingers are like chipolatas,
Me!
My chest is like a bucket,
Me!
My stomach is like a molehill,
Me!
My legs are like wooden stakes,
Me!
My feet are like long rectangular shoeboxes,
Me!
My back is like a plank of wood,
Me!

Thomas Biegel (11)
Colchester High School

TIME FLIES WHEN YOU'RE IN LOVE

Why did I let it go?
I thought time was moving slow,
But when I checked, it had gone,
And along with it,
Went my heart.

Was it a one hit wonder
Or was it gonna go further?
I didn't even have time
To stop and stare,
Into your eyes.

Why didn't I stop and think?
I think I was on the brink,
Of getting closer to you,
And touching your lips
With mine.

Oh well, what can I say?
I hope I see you another day,
I hope you are always well and okay
By yourself.

Now I'm all alone
When I'm at home,
Apart from my folks,
I hope I see another bloke,
Who is as good as you.

Time flies when you're in love,
Has that ever happened to you?

Kayleigh Watson (12)
Dagenham Priory Comprehensive School

WHERE DO ALL THE TEACHERS GO?

Where do all the teachers go
When it's 4 o'clock?
Do they live in houses
And do they wash their socks?

Do they wear pyjamas
And do they watch TV?
And do they pick their noses
The same as you and me?

Do they live with older people?
Have they mums and dads?
And were they ever children
And were they ever bad?

Did they ever lose their hymn books?
Did they ever leave their greens?
Did they ever scribble on the desktops?
Did they ever wear old dirty jeans?

I'll follow one back home today
I'll find out what they do
Then I'll put it in a poem
That they can read to you.

Patience A Grugglsberg (14)
Dagenham Priory Comprehensive School

ESCAPING FROM WAR

Escaping from war in an air balloon.
With a gas bottle to help us
Reach the moon.
Ropes dangling everywhere
Red to show despair

It looks like blood
It's mixed with mud
War on a battleground
Year 2050, war is still around
Boy and girl get away
Freedom for another day.

Bill Ruel (13)
Dagenham Priory Comprehensive School

I WISH THE WORLD WOULD BE A BETTER PLACE

I wish the world could be a better place,
and so many things I'd like to face.
Africa, Asia and many more
Those helpless countries are very poor.

I wish there were a thousand bins
so our streets and homes would be the cleanest things.
Let the dustmen do their jobs,
so fill the bins and don't be slobs.

Don't forget homeless people on the streets,
hungry and smelly, dragging their dirty feet.
They need food and money and a place to stay,
so please help them and make their day.

If all these things in my poem were done,
this world would be the only one
to love and cherish a precious place,
so correct this world face-to-face.

Genevieve Smith (12)
Dagenham Priory Comprehensive School

OUT OF THE DARKNESS

I walk among the trees
Isolated, scared and unsure.
Nothing to hear but the rustle of the wind,
Voices whispering among the leaves.

The silent wood is dark and gloomy.
Blurred shapes, like strange shadows
Surrounding me, closing me in.

In the distance a tiny light
Breaks through the darkness,
Showing me the path
Guiding me the right way.

I see a light,
I rush towards it as it gleams through me
Leaving desperation behind,
Knowing that special God was
There beside me.

Charlotte Golding (12)
Friends' School

THE OWL

If you creep into the forest at night,
Beware! Be ready for a fearsome fright,
For high above, amongst the trees,
There waits a creature masked by leaves,
Who sits and stares at prey below,
And listens in silence, so you can't know
What danger lingers there.

And there it is, without a clue,
Before the sun has warmed the dew,
The madly-screeching sounds of thrill,
With swiftly swooping claws, the kill.
The owl, at last, has had its prey,
And again can hide, from light of day.
He's sleeping now till the dead of night,
Stay away! Or you may give *him* a fright.

Fergus Walsh (11)
Friends' School

THE STORM

The rain crashed on the window.
The road flooded with showering water.
Splish, splosh, went the loud rain banging
furiously in every road or lane around me.

The wind tore down the window frame,
knocking at the shutters,
trumpeting and screaming through the small
cracks in the floorboards.

Lightning stomped, shaking everything in the room.
Striking, banging, crashing, as though
stamping around on a hollow wall.

The storm started to blow over; then
there was just a small snuffle as the rain
slowly drifted away.

Camilla Oelman (11)
Friends' School

SEPTEMBER 11TH

A day of sadness, a day of shock,
A day when reality came to an end.

You feel horror from photos and film
And grieve over what the world has come to,
But think how you would feel
If you were inside, caught unaware.

You are in an elevator shaft:
You're trapped and know nothing of what is going on around you.
You are worried, but fear has not struck you yet.

You are at work:
A crash, a bang and smoke.
Suddenly you realise you have to get out before it's too late.

You are in a stairwell:
You are terrified.
It all seems surreal.
You push and shove.
No one else matters, but you.

You are on the top floor:
You are stuck.
Pure fear follows you.
Terror hangs over the building.
You can't get out; it is simply impossible.

What do you do?
Do you wait for death to take you?
Do you make an attempt to save yourself?
Do you jump and know you will not see the end?

Your life is at stake.

You can only think one thing:

Fear!

Kenya Brading (11)
Friends' School

DREAMING OF HORSES!

Galloping, cantering, across the meadows,
His muscles ripple as he gallops,
Brown shimmering coat,
A wild nature running free,
Rearing, bucking, as the night draws in,
He settles down in a warm, cosy stable,
Dreaming of roaming free,
Oh, how I wish he was mine,
Riding through the woods.

Christie Wright (12)
Great Baddow High School

My Emotions

My fear is like a shivering iceberg.
My love is like a fiery lava pit.
My madness is like a furious tornado.
My envy is like a tranquil ocean.
My jealousy is like a burning fire, killing me.
My happiness is like a smiling sun, shining down.
My sadness is like a lonely desert, waiting to be found.
My peace is like a drizzling waterfall.
My guilt is like an avalanche.
My loneliness is like a deserted jungle.
My warmth is like a bubbling volcano.

These are my emotions.

Becky Breedon (11)
Great Baddow High School

My Emotions

My strength is like a deadly sea,
My crying is like a running waterfall,
My anger is like an exploding volcano,
My sadness is like a silent ocean,
My happiness is like a noisy jungle,
My confidence is like a growing glacier,
My loneliness is like an echoing valley,
My fury is like a burning sun,
My jealously is like a furious sea,
My fear is like a tingly iceberg.

These are my emotions.

Brendon Farrelly (12)
Great Baddow High School

MY GONE PUPPY

My puppy, joyful as ever,
playing in the garden,
but why, oh why, did my little sister
let him run away?
I chased after him.
He had been let out of the front door.
He went out on the road.
A car came and didn't see the fluffy puppy
and now he's gone.
When he got run over he cried and howled.
I screamed and fell on my knees.
If only my sister hadn't let him out,
he wouldn't be gone.
I would still hear him.
If only my sister hadn't let him out,
he wouldn't be dead on the road.

Anna Manfredi (11)
Great Baddow High School

MY EMOTIONS

My fear is like a strong hurricane.
My love is like a deep ocean.
My jealousy is like a smelly jungle.
My faith is like a flowing universe.
My strength is like a small mountain.
My sadness is like a rainy sea.
My anger is like a spitting volcano.
My pain is like a cut-down tree.
My madness is like a boiling countryside.

Sophie Cannon (11)
Great Baddow High School

BROKEN HEART

As I lie in wonder,
Watching the minutes go by,
I think of you but do you think of I?
As my eyes slowly drift,
My lips whisper the words,
'I'll always love you.'
Now my life is over
I shall think of you way up in Heaven
But I will always be there at the
                bottom of your heart,
I want you to know and remember
I shall be waiting for the day
                we're together again.

Jade Woulfe (11)
Great Baddow High School

MY EMOTIONS

My sadness is like an ongoing stream,
My anger is like an exploding volcano,
My happiness is like the shining sun,
My love is like a sparkling waterfall,
My pain is like a splitting iceberg,
My envy is like a green tree,
My faith is like a strong wall,
My boredom is like a wandering path,
My fear is like a high mountain,
My strength is like a fierce wind,
My jealousy is like a raging river.

These are my emotions.

Louise Thomas (11)
Great Baddow High School

MY EMOTIONS

My envy is like a green sea,
My love is like a blazing fire,
My fear is like a wild boar,
My sorrow is like a marshy swamp,
My horror is like a white iceberg,
My guilt is like a desert island,
My desire is like an orange sun,
My joy is like a calm stream,
My peace is like a bendy meander,
My pain is like a strong hailstorm,
My boredom is like a rainy day,
My pity is like a sad graveyard,
My jealousy is like a grey-green sky,
My anger is like a raging hurricane.

These are my emotions.

Paul Beard (11)
Great Baddow High School

MY EMOTIONS

My anger is like a raging tornado.
My fury is like an exploding volcano.
My love is like a deep ocean.
My guilt is like a hot desert.
My happiness is like a fluffy cloud.
My fear is like a freezing glacier.
My pain is like a slashing sea.
My sadness is like a dead jungle.
My fury is like an action-packed city.
My pity is like a dying plant.

These are my emotions.

Carys Kyei (11)
Great Baddow High School

MY EMOTIONS

My anger is like an exploding volcano
My fear is like a flaming river
My hatred is like a raging tornado
My quilt is like a bubbling lava pit
My envy is like a smashing hurricane
My happiness is like a flowing waterfall
My boredom is like a hot desert
My madness is like a fierce lightning storm
My sadness is like a wandering ocean
My spite is like a slashing sea
My love is like a swift stream
My joy is like a fluffy cloud
My shame is like a dead tree
My pity is like a dying plant
My jealousy is like a howling wolf.

These are my emotions!

Tommy Ecott (11)
Great Baddow High School

RAIN

Rain and sun, makes a rainbow,
it trickles away as happily as can be.
Splash! Splash!
Crash! Crash!
As children slip over,
their parents get mad and clean away,
they say they are angry but don't
really mean it!

Daniel Filby (11)
Great Baddow High School

MY EMOTIONS

My quietness is like a calm countryside,
My happiness is like a glittering waterfall,
My anger is like a hot volcano,
My envy is like a green ocean,
My guilt is like a dark sky,
My madness is like a fast boulder,
My pain is like a freezing glacier,
My hate is like a boiling lava pit,
My love is like a wild fire,
My sadness is like a dark cave,
My jealousy is like a raging hurricane,
My sorrow is like a lonely star,
My boredom is like a black hole,
My fear is like a cold mountain,

These are my emotions.

Camille Collinson
Great Baddow High School

MY EMOTIONS

My envy is like a deadly volcano,
My happiness is like a calm ocean,
My faith is like a quiet forest,
My pain is like a raging hurricane,
My anger is like a boiling lava pit,
My jealousy is like an exploding gun,
My pity is like a lonely moon,
My guilt is like a deep waterfall,
My spite is like a strong wind,
My sadness is like a smooth sea,

These are my emotions.

Jake Cochrane (11)
Great Baddow High School

MY EMOTIONS

My happiness is like soft, white sand,
My joy is like white snow,
My madness is like a busy city,
My strength is like terrible rocks,
My envy is like a dry desert,
My jealousy is like a baking sun,
My anger is like a bubbling volcano,
My hatred is like hard rain,
My spite is like sharp stones,
My hate is like a deep, dark crater,
My guilt is like a raging storm,
My faith is like a white cloud,
My fear is like a flash of lightning,
My pain is like a speared deer,
My regret is like a never-ending path,
My worry is like a wet rainforest,
My loneliness is like a tall, snowy mountain,
My woe is like dirty world pollution,
My pity is like a wandering stream,
My sorrow is like an overgrown jungle,
My boredom is like small, round pebbles,
My sadness is like a bottomless hole.

These are my emotions.

Daniel Looney (11)
Great Baddow High School

WHERE HAS MY LOVELY DOG GONE?

My cute dog, Carlo, had to be put down,
All he liked to do was walk around and sniff the ground,
When he was young, he always went out for a run,
But gradually, as he got older, he couldn't even lift his tum!

My poor, sad, Cavalier King Charles, had a really cute face,
His fluffy body was warm and soft and as smooth as lace,
He would curl up at night and gently fall asleep,
But now he is gone!

Olivia Chitty (11)
Great Baddow High School

THE POUNCE

The green eyes watched me through the window of the house,
And like a mouse I crept along the path,
The green eyes belonged to a cat,
It looked a little fat,
And it was creepy.
I walked a little faster,
But I bumped into the master,
The giant master of the cats,
I ran.
I ran as fast as I could go.
I seemed to run a little slow,
But still I ran.
Oops! I tripped over the can
The one that was once drunk by me,
And there it came,
The pounce!
Could I be dead?
But how could I have said
This poem?

Holly Weeks (11)
Great Baddow High School

THE MOST TRAGIC DAY EVER!

Today is a tragic day,
The Twin Towers collapsed,
Some planes hit the tower,
Everyone was panicking,
From streets, windows and the tower.

Lots of people left someone behind,
It was the worst day ever,
Thousands of people were killed for no reason,
Everyone was upset by this,

Millions of rescuers risked their lives,
Trying to find and get people out to safety,
But they couldn't get many people out,

There are a lot of memories about the people who died,
Everyone will remember them, especially their families and friends,
They wish they could see them again,
But sadly they won't ever see them again!

Samantha Knott (11)
Great Baddow High School

THE SUN

The sun is up in the sky
It's very bright, it makes me cry
And sometimes it makes me sneeze.
My hanky is covered in cream cheese.

One day it may be grey and the sun might go away
But that might not be such a crime
Because Mum won't know it's bedtime.

Victoria Roberts (11)
Great Baddow High School

MY GRANDAD'S LIFE

My grandad liked watching videos, especially cowboy ones.
My grandad always made people laugh, no matter how he was feeling.
My grandad had an allotment in which he used to grow lots of
                                                green beans.
My grandad always went to watch football on Sunday morning
                                          over at Danbury Park.
My grandad's favourite dinner was definitely roast.
My grandad used to work on motorways, tarmacking.
My grandad was very strong because he was always in hospital.
My grandad liked to go down the pub to have a pint or two.
My grandad was very well-known because he spoke to everyone.
My grandad lived in Danbury all his life.
My grandad died of cancer in his sleep.
Best of all my grandad supported Tottenham Hotspurs.

Joe Collins (11)
Great Baddow High School

THE TRAGEDY OF 9/11

I was just minding my own business,
When all of a sudden
I heard an almighty explosion.
Of course, I looked up,
My eyes were drawn to the Twin Towers,
I was surprised!
You couldn't see the South Tower through all the smoke,
Or hear yourself think for all the screaming.
I wanted to run, run far away from this dreadful place,
I tried to run but I couldn't,
It seemed that my feet were rooted to the spot.
Then *boom!* A plane crashed, into the North Tower!

Stephen White (11)
Great Baddow High School

My Emotions

My sorrow is like a calm stream,
My meanness is like a boiling lava pit,
My madness is like a wild jungle,
My happiness is like a sweet lake.

My hatred is like a rapid sea,
My anger is like an exploding volcano,
My fear is like a ginormous mountain,
My strength is like a fierce, twisting hurricane.

My love is like a beautiful waterfall,
My envy is like a deadly rocket,
My temper is like a raging asteroid,

These are my emotions.

Daniel Bruce (11)
Great Baddow High School

The Mayor And The Spider

There is a spider on a chair,
In comes the mayor,
Squashes the spider square,
And falls down the stairs.

The spider builds a web,
The mayor walks in the shed,
The mayor gets tangled up,
And the spider gets a golden cup.

The mayor has a final run,
And catches the spider in a bun,
Pours himself a drink of rum,
And then makes a silent hum.

Edward Rendell (11)
Great Baddow High School

MY FRIEND DAN

My friend Dan was a close friend
He was kind and happy
He was always smiling
Dan always had a joke to tell.

But he sadly fell ill
He wasn't getting better
We all kept our hopes up
Dan went into hospital

He had cancer
He had an operation to remove it

It was successful at first
He went through about two weeks
Before he had to go back to hospital

It wasn't long before the cancer came back
He became weaker and weaker
Still our hopes were even higher

Dan fought it off as long as he could
It sadly beat him and he died
I will never forget him as he was a special friend
A truthful friend
He was my friend.

At his memorial the boys sang, 'I'll be missing you'
And the girls sang, 'I'll say a little prayer for you'.
I will never ever forget him.

Greg Flinders (12)
Great Baddow High School

MY EMOTIONS

My anger is like a spinning tornado
My sadness is like a cold glacier
My hate is like a boiling volcano
My boredom is like an empty desert
My envy is like a green sea
My guilt is like a bubbling lava pit
My happiness is like a trickling stream
My love is like a big ocean
My pain is like a speeding river
My sorrow is like a lonely cave
My madness is like a terrorising hurricane
My faith is like a widening estuary

These are my emotions.

Neil Searles (11)
Great Baddow High School

LOSING A MEMBER OF THE FAMILY

When I saw the morning gloom,
I knew something was wrong.
I went downstairs to watch tele,
and my sister came running, crying,
She said 'The rabbit's dead.'
I felt a shock down my back.
I felt really sad, it was like losing
a member of the family.
As I went to bed that night all I could see
was my rabbit staring me in the eye.

James Goddard (11)
Great Baddow High School

MY EMOTIONS

My anger is like a burning fire
My love is like a flowing river
My strength is like a hard hurricane
My boredom is like a boiling volcano
My madness is like an exploding sun
My fear is like a silent lake
My happiness is like an exciting star
My pain is like a sharp mountain
My bossiness is like a dangerous tornado
My guilt is like a splashing ocean
My jealousy is like a dark green creeper
My faith is like a running waterfall
My hatred is like a raging lava pit.

These are my emotions.

Shane Bone (11)
Great Baddow High School

MY DOG, PEBBLES

I lost my dog a few months ago,
She was a beautiful white boxer
She was sweet, cute and very funny
She was six when she died
She loved children and running away
She used to run away down to the park
She died because she had a brain tumour
I cried and I cried
It doesn't matter how much I cry
It won't bring her back.

Liberty Donald (11)
Great Baddow High School

A Lost Friend

My friend was a special guy, he was one of a kind,
now he's gone.
I feel so empty, like a piece of me is missing.
I will never forget the day he departed from me
by moving away, now I fear I will never see him again.
Even though I know it will be a new experience
I wish he didn't have to go.
I wish I had spent more time with him, getting to know him better.
My friend, such a caring, understanding person,
great for a laugh.
I hope he won't forget me.
I expect he will make new friends,
But I hope our friendship never ends.

My friend Josh.

Sam Haldane (11)
Great Baddow High School

The Storm

I woke up one morning hearing a loud noise,
I looked out my window and saw the storm,
The lightning was so bright it hurt my eyes,
The noise was ferocious,
And with it, lightning destroying street lights.

The rain was horrendous, it nearly flooded the whole town,
It was very black with a dark grey sky,
The lightning was beaming brightly,
It was a horrible storm to look at!

James Hall (11)
Great Baddow High School

MY EMOTIONS

My hate is like a roaring river of flames,
My loneliness is like a wandering stream,
My pain is like dead trees,
My strength is like a fierce hurricane,
My fear is like a terrifying thunderstorm,
My anger is like a bubbling spring,
My boredom is like a still lake,
My pity is like an abandoned village,
My energy is like a burning star,
My sorrow is like a vandalised town,
My love is like a wild forest fire,
My pride is like a strong lion,
My jealousy is like an ignored building,

These are my emotions.

Jack Venn (11)
Great Baddow High School

KAYLEIGH

Kayleigh, Kayleigh, the blonde in your hair,
Makes me feel like a pear,
Ripening on a tree.

Kayleigh, Kayleigh, the blue in your eyes,
Makes me lie,
Saying I don't love you.

Kayleigh, Kayleigh, the beauty in your face,
Makes you look so cute
Like a puppy.

Kayleigh, Kayleigh, I count the days till you're mine.

Michael Regan (11)
Great Baddow High School

THE 9/11 TRAGEDY

A tragedy occurs,
Lots of firemen,
Drive their fire engines,
To the Twin Towers,
Lots of people worried,
Aeroplanes into the side of the Towers,
I hear screams,
Lots of fire and smoke,
Enormous explosions,
People panicking,
Buildings crashing to the ground.
Fireman risk their lives,
They bravely enter the building,
Gallons of water,
Being tipped on the Twin Towers,
Lots of people running,
Terrified about the event
That is happening,
North Tower collapsing
To the ground,
But shortly after,
South Tower comes
Crumbling down,
Lots of dads being missed,
Women becoming widows
As their families come to an end.

Ryan Baxter (12)
Great Baddow High School

MY EMOTIONS

My hatred is like a boiling lava pit,
My happiness is like a sparkling waterfall,
My jealousy is like a hot sun,
My boredom is like a dull grey sky,
My sadness is like a silent village,
My anger is like a bubbling volcano,
My envy is like a cold glacier,
My fear is like a terrifying thunderstorm,
My pain is like a dead plant,
My strength is like a tall tree,
My spite is like a raging animal,
My guilt is like a wandering meander,
My sorrow is like a poor town,
My pity is like a small country,
My energy is like a flowing river,

These are my emotions.

Matt Skeoch
Great Baddow High School

CLOUDS

Clouds are like cheetahs speeding through the air.
Clouds can rage up like a ferocious shark.
Clouds can vanish like birds in winter.
Clouds can build up like an ever-growing city.
Clouds can land like a plane.
Clouds are light-keepers because they let light out
                                        or hold it in.

Adam Hone (12)
Great Baddow High School

THE DINOSAUR

As he runs,
it sounds like guns,
running at full steam.
As they work as a team,
they jump really high,
they look like they can fly.
As they search for prey
you never hear what they'll say.
As they hunt prey down with speed
they are too fast to read,
At the end of the run
the deed has been done.
(Who am I?)

Answer: A velociraptor.

Steven Riley (12)
Great Baddow High School

THE DEVIL

The Devil,
Blood-red, covered in fire,
Giving off a stench,
Like sulphur but immeasurably stronger,
His eyes like knives piercing deep into your soul,
There is no remorse
Or fear,
Only the evil that he is,

> *The Devil!*

James Edwards (12)
Hassenbrook GM School

THE BEGINNING OF THE DEVIL

The wind poisoned the air
The quiet night was gone
The man stood there, sightless he may have been
His trumpet woke the angels of God

Tears rolled down the man's cheek
The Devil was near
And the sight of life to come
Was surely not going to be there
The creation of the Devil had begun
The host, so quiet
He had the knife of the dead.

Jonathan Shovlar (15)
Hassenbrook GM School

THE ANTARCTIC

Spectacular ice,
on a snowy, cold mountain,
as the sun rises.

Pearl-white glacier,
you shine in the sunlit day,
proud of where you are.

Shiny icicle,
pointy, sharp as a needle,
but you're liked that way.

Eliott Farr (11)
Hassenbrook GM School

THE HOMELESS

The homeless live on the streets,
The homeless sit on the roadsides,
The homeless sleep in the doorways of shops,
The homeless live alone, afraid.

How long have they been there?
How long will they stay?
How do they cope?
How do they feel?

Jeered at by the ignorant who don't understand,
By those who don't want to know them.
By those who don't realise how unfortunate they are . . .
By those who just don't care.

They want a job, they want a friend,
They want a life, they want a future.
They want a home, they want a family,
They want to know they're loved.

They need to know that someone cares,
They need enough money, just to get by.
They need a friend to help them through,
They need the safety of a home.

Do you ever think about how they feel?
Do you ever think about why they're there?
Do you ever think about what they must go through?
Do you ever think about them at all?

Have they ever known life in a home?
Have they ever known the warmth of a bed?
Have they ever known a merry Christmas?
Have they ever known the love from a family?

Were they drawn to the city searching for hope?
Were they expecting to find a well-paid job?
Were they drawn to the city searching for hope?
But did they find it, in the end?

Did they walk out on their family?
Did they argue a lot?
Did they walk out on their family
Were the arguments too painful to stay?

Have they lived on the streets all their life?
Have they not known any different?
Have they lived on the streets all their life?
Do they ever feel secure?

The homeless live on the streets,
The homeless sit on the roadsides,
The homeless sleep in the doorways of shops,
The homeless live alone, afraid.

Chloe Flame (13)
Hassenbrook GM School

THE OLD MAN FROM FRANCE

There was an old man from France,
He went to the beach to dance,
He hurt his knee and fell in the sea,
And was washed up in Africa by chance!

Daisy Flame (11)
Hassenbrook GM School

I Am Your Spirit

Part 1

I am the spirit in the sky
Controlling what's below me
I am the concrete in the ground
Holding up what's above me.
I am the angel inside of you
Helping everyone around me.
I am the life that makes you up
I help you to control me.

You are the person that inspires me
That is why I chose you.
I'll support you through thick and thin
No matter what you do
If you use me and abuse me
I'll fight you all the way
There is nothing that can hurt me
I am here to stay.

I can't stop you doing things
The things you want to do
I'll fight for you but I can't die for you
I am here to stay
I am your spirit, I am your guide
And when you die I'll be by your side
When you die is when I leave you
I'm nothing but a spirit.

Part 2 Evil side to the story

I am the controlling demon
Who gave you sins when born.
I lived under your mother's feet
- Deeper than that maybe.
I am the Devil inside you
I make you misbehave
I'm the 'thing' that makes you unpure
The 'thing' that makes you bad.

You looked like an easy target
You looked vulnerable and naïve
I will make you live my perfect life
Causing havoc wherever I stand.
You can never use me or abuse me
- Just fulfil my needs - whatever they may be
There is nothing that can hurt me
I am here, you can't get rid of me.

I will make you do the things
- The things you wish to do
I will fight with you and for you
I am infecting your innocence
I am your friend, I'll be second-best.
I'll give you the best (and worst!) days of your life
When you die I'll drag you down
So you can live a life of evil for eternity with me.

Victoria Sallows (15)
Hassenbrook GM School

Untitled

Don't you realise that you're blind?
The natural world is all in your mind,
Nature is your creation,
Behind the blanket of your eye
There is no light.
Horror and ghosts are beset by night,
Go ahead, take a look
The world is not a pretty book.

You believe that all is well
The visions you see are just fairy tales
Please open your eyes
You're treading on nails.

Wicked dreams you see is the real reality
I am trapped
So are you
Evil vs Good is making me blue.

Shall I take the blade
And separate the ghost from my body?
I'm tired of the truth.
Murder is the only way out
I've got nothing to lose.

I think of the world as I once knew
It's now gone and so am I as
I take my last cold breath and head for the sky.

Many a time,
Wicked dreams have filled my thoughtless mind,
When I dream, nature is just a creation and,
Horror is as real as a vision.

As I sleep my creation of murder and ghosts
Becomes reality.
For me, all good has abandoned my hopeless mind,
Wickedness has taken over
And the cold breath of which I breathe
Is getting colder.

These dreams from which, I usually awake
The visions are still cut deep inside my head.
It is giving me a sign.
Do I dare take the blade?
The blade which I shall use to dispose of
This wicked mind of mine
For I have sinned.

My mistakes haunt my mind
I don't want to be bad, when I try to be good
I do something evil
Please give me peace.

Jade Gibbs (14)
Hassenbrook GM School

JUST THINKING

I sat peacefully on the soft, sand dunes. I could just see
a small, red, sailing ship out on the distant horizon.
I could lightly hear the sound of the sneaky, seagulls behind,
The song of the beautiful, calm, blue sea
Running gently over the cold, grey stones and rocks . . .

I sat thinking!

Karris Rowbotham (11)
Hassenbrook GM School

LOVE

Love is such a strange emotion,
Because true love is so hard to find.
You can like someone very much,
But it always seems to end.

Love can be quite terrible,
It can end a friendship sent from Heaven.
The wonderful feeling starts with good intentions,
But it often ends in resentment.

Love often influences the downfall of close chums,
Resulting with jealousy and conflict.
However, all love does not shatter,
True love can be found where hearts are strong and forgiving.

Love brings together unforeseen couples,
It ties a bond between two lovers,
Love can last for eternity,
With lots of love, trust and care.

Love is a strange emotion,
Because true love is so hard to find,
You can like someone very much,
But it always seems to end.

Hannah Southgate (13)
Hassenbrook GM School

SENSES

I can see the colours of the rainbow,
And I can hear the soft singing of birds.
I can feel the heat from the sun high above,
I can taste the apples, ripe from the tree,
And I can smell the sweet scent of coloured flowers.

I can see the reflection of me in the mirror,
And I can hear the laughter of happy children.
I can feel the softness of a teddy bear,
I can taste my toast, hot from the toaster,
And I can smell the fresh morning air.

Kayleigh North (13)
Hassenbrook GM School

THE DAY THE WORLD CRIED

The towers fell,
This caused the world to be outraged Hell,
People crying,
And the terrorists lying,

What a day it was,

No one will forget,
Nor America be in debt,
The terrorists should be in shame,
Because that day caused so much pain,

What a day it was,

A lot of lives taken,
And millions more shaken,
A lot of bodies laid to rest,
This day could never have been guessed,

What a day that was,

September the 11th, 2001

A day never to be forgotten by the world.

Natasha Wareham (14)
Hassenbrook GM School

THE TRIP THAT KILLED ME

This is a fine ship, I thought to myself as we set sail,
Along the river into the wide open sea,
On the maiden voyage,
What were we going to see?
They said this ship is the best and will never sink,
But what are they to know?
On board, everyone celebrated the launch,
Everything seemed so fine, as we passed out of port onto the open sea.
It glided through the water like a dolphin in a race,
'Three cheers for the Titanic' announced the captain over the speakers,
While going along the river into the wide open sea.

A week had gone, it was quiet now,
The sights were fantastic as we headed up towards the Arctic.
'Iceberg ahead!' the captain shouted in an air of panic,
Which sent the passengers into a frenzy.
All around children shouting, screaming, crying,
Men and women cuddled together as this became their last hours alive.
From below the stern came a great screech as she collided
with the natural obstacle,
Ice-cold water flooded in through the gap drowning crew
as they worked.

It was four minutes before the great wonder tipped her rudders
into the air,
As if she was waving a hopeless surrender.
People fell great distances before hitting an ice-cold death,
Lifeboats floated around, some half-empty,
Others overloaded.
Some survived.
I didn't.

Now I regret, regret having a birthday present that killed me.
As I sit up here, looking down,
I shed a tear, wanting to be alive again, to have fun,
To dance, sing and drink.
Oh I wish that I had never taken that trip,
The trip that killed me.

Aaron Gouge (15)
Hassenbrook GM School

WAR GAMES

Laser shots that singe the air,
They've got more troops than us, that's not fair!

Plasma shots will melt your armour,
They can also really harm ya!

Gruesome aliens that crush a head!
Oh my God, my best friend's dead!

Mutant zombies eat our brains,
Then suck blood from out our veins!

Superhuman warriors force us into cover,
Hey! You just shot my brother!

Bombs explode and take us apart,
Then aliens drive over us in a ten-ton cart!

We fought bravely but lost the war,
Having no weapons was our major flaw!

Our army general was a panto dame,
Lucky this was just a game!

Daniel Skinner (14)
Hassenbrook GM School

MY CURE

I awoke this morning at six o'clock,
Just before the light of day,
I rose with warmth and such contentment,
In a funny sort of way.

At first I thought, *what am I doing?*
I usually rise at a later time,
But then I looked out of my window,
My timing was good, in fact just fine.

The scenery that, at first, I saw,
Was quite pleasing to my eyes,
I then looked out, out to sea,
And saw it, it was sunrise.

The colours were so beautiful,
I stood there still, stood in awe,
The beautiful colours blended finely,
Even the blues and whites of the shore.

As I stood there staring out to sea,
I thought about the days before,
They surely were tragic but I felt happy,
That was it, I'd found my cure.

After days of so much pain,
Things were different, through my eyes,
I had learnt my lesson, it had taught me well,
The beauty of it, of the sunrise.

Natalie Godward (14)
Hassenbrook GM School

THERE IS A SHAPE

There is a shape on the cliff top,
A shape that no one really knows,
With its head held high,
With its tail down low,
And its sound,
A cry.

Where does it go in the daytime?
The paw prints do not tell,
Where does it go on the cold winter nights?
Does the family follow?
And its sound,
A cry.

It seems to disappear in the hunting season,
When the snow turns red with blood,
The other animals seem to follow it,
Between morning and between dusk,
And its sound,
A cry.

This mysterious creature,
Who stands on the cliff top,
Has let its secret go,
When the wind is blowing over the cool white snow,
It is clear,
Its sound,
A cry of a wolf.

Joanna Pemberton (14)
Hassenbrook GM School

DEFINITION OF A TRAGEDY

What is this I see before
my eyes?
What can I do?
Will this be me in the future or is this the shadows
of the past now gone?

What do they do
Their world now shattered?
What can I do
With my world before me?
What do they do
Their world now shattered?
What can I do
With my world before me?

Why do they run?
Why do they hide?
In a world of misery where they
now live.
Will I slip into this world
or will my world submerge into dreams?

A fissure in my life
a fissure in the city
where once the Twins stood
now a labyrinth of ruins.

I mourn for their loss
I feel the hate rise up in me
Inside my shell I wait
and bleed.

Shaun McIntosh (14)
Hassenbrook GM School

I MUST LEARN

What is this world
Into which I have just been born?
I want to know,
I want to learn.

I am told
To watch a screen,
And what I see,
Is just destruction.

I see people
With water dripping from their eyes,
Why, I ask,
Are they broken?

I see more people
Who must be broken also,
They leak a red liquid,
Surrounded by burning buildings.

And now I see
A vehicle moving through the air,
A recurring image,
Showing it hitting, over and over,
Not one but two tall buildings,
They are like twins.

And now it shows the aftermath,
Falling . . . falling . . . the building goes down,
A tremendous roar of solid against solid.
It is, no more.

Adam Bulpitt (13)
Hassenbrook GM School

My Grandad And Me

He was wise to his time,
And was never unkind,
He always made me happy,
I'm so glad he's mine.

He helped me with my maths,
When it was hard,
I continue to remember, those methods he gave,
In tests I just think of him, he makes me feel brave.

When I was sad and down inside,
I would run and hide,
But he was always there for me,
For warmth and company.

When I came home there was a shock for me,
I couldn't have my grandad's company.
I heard the bad news from my mum and dad,
It made me curl up,
Upset and sad.

About a month later he came out of hospital,
I went to see him; it made me feel glad.
He checked on my tables, before I said goodbye.
I hugged him and felt a warmth inside.

In the morning, I had the biggest shock.
The worst news had come to me.
I was eating my breakfast when my dad said,
'Your grandad died in his warm bed.'

I will never forget his kindness and warmth,
I will always know that he will love me,
And it will always be,
My Grandad and me.

Vicky Abbott (13)
Hassenbrook GM School

The Ballerina

Graceful, minute steps glide across with care,

Soft, elegant music fills sweet-smelling air,

Legs like flowing ribbon, moving effortlessly around,

Body, stretching all ways possible, yet still I hear not a sound.

Soft silky slippers, worn but worn with care,

Everything so perfect, not least her pinned-back hair,

Performance finishes, silence, audience clap in awe,

The ballerina waits, and then leaves the dance floor.

Marie Sorenson (15)
Hassenbrook GM School

The Magic Book!

Found in abandoned library,
Scales of dragon on cover,
Skeleton spine.

Magical face on front not moving,
Begins to move,
Moves mouth.

English knight comes out mouth,
Raises sword above head.

One big swing of sword,
Off with limbs and you're dead.

James Cummings (12)
Hassenbrook GM School

Anger And Pain

Why so much anger?
Why so much pain?
All the wars
All the greed
Two buildings to fall
Yet nothing to gain.

Why so much anger?
Why so much pain?
All the poverty
All the racism
As the Falklands are won
We count the cost of death.

Why so much anger?
Why so much pain?
All the hunger
All the pollution
As speed becomes a danger
Death becomes apparent.

Matt Sandy (13)
Hassenbrook GM School

The Book

Dingy, mystical, forgotten shop,
Unicorn horns, werewolf fangs,
Wizened man, wizard's hat,
Eye caught shiny book.

Turquoise waters, moving waves,
Golden sun, glints magnificently,
Dolphins leap, whales glide,
Through sapphire-blue waters.

Reach touch hand sinks,
Hand plunges, icy water,
Falling, falling, falling, falling,
Rushing sensation, light air.

Beautiful island, amazing sight
Green hills, babbling brooks,
Golden sands, lapping waters,
Wonderful place, never leave.

Charlotte Brainwood (12)
Hassenbrook GM School

TWINS

A tragic moment.
Feeling distressed, alarmed,
Going from transparent to opaque,
From bright to dark.

The Twin Towers were there once
Reaching up to the skies,
That day changed our world
And you could see the shock in people's eyes.

Every country was touched by sadness.
The Americans were not alone.
Thousands of lives were lost.
Buried under tonnes of rubble and dust.

Memories still with us,
As we overlook the past,
The 11th September
Will never be forgotten.

Lettie Nice (13)
Hassenbrook GM School

THROUGH MY WINDOW

I look out my window, I wonder what's out there?
Danger, terror, all the things that scare me.

As I glance through the glass,
all kinds of thoughts run through my mind.

Like on September 11th, a time no one will forget.
People who have lost someone they love
and some still trying to find that special someone.

People boarding a train, thinking it will be a normal journey,
but who can be certain that that's all it will be?

I look out my window, I take a good look at
some of the nice things that happen,

Like when we give and receive gifts
and donate our time to charity,
that is what makes our world a better place.

Who knows what will become of this world in years to come?
Maybe a world of lies and deceit. Or even a world of love and hope,
but sadly I may never know!

Sophie Allison (13)
Hassenbrook GM School

THE TOOTH FAIRY

Tooth Fairy, Tooth Fairy, where have you been?
Are you riding under the sea in a submarine?
Cos I have a tooth which is shiny and clean,
Please come tonight, you won't be seen,
And you'll always be a beautiful creature to me.

Samantha Barnett (11)
Hassenbrook GM School

FEELINGS

I feel happiness,
I feel glee,
Today, nothing can sadden me,
Because I'm happy as a lark,
Bright as the sun,
I hope to bring cheerfulness to everyone.

I feel depressed,
I feel sad,
Everything in my life seems so bad.
I don't feel happy, not one bit,
Feeling blue, that's me,
Can anything end my misery?

I feel relaxed,
I feel calm,
The whole world is in my palm.
I'm not nervous,
I can take on anything,
Ready for whatever life brings.

I feel anger,
I feel hate,
I want revenge, just you wait.
Because I've lost my patience,
And I'm so annoyed,
If you weren't here, I'd be overjoyed.

Stress, sadness, anger, hate,
Peace, love, happiness and glee,
These are all the feelings of me.
Some feelings are dark as night,
Others bright as day.
How do you feel today?

Hannah Shilling (13)
Hassenbrook GM School

A Loss Of My Own

Day after day,
I see no returning,
I need to find another way
To carry on, on my own.

        The tragic event,
        The day still haunts me,
        If only I could prevent
        This loss of my own.

How can anybody push themselves so far
To use a plane as a terrorist tool?
Never in my wildest dreams,
Because of this, I'm on my own.

        The impact was mighty,
        The smoke, dyeing New York's skyline,
        All problems were left behind,
        Because I have no problems, on my own.

The smoke bellowed
For a mere hour,
The Tower wounded to its heart,
Without her, trapped inside, I'm all alone,

        Suddenly, silence fell amongst the world
        Everyone was brought to their knees,
        As one, then two, mountains collapsed,
        Leaving loved ones on their own,

But what did that person responsible care?
Tearing my life apart,
The pain and deceit, I can feel,
An empty space inside.

I can no longer bear this loss,
A loss so close to me,
And so many others around the world,
Who lost someone on this day.
But for now I'll have to live,
With this loss of my own,
With no one to love, no one to care,
Because my mother was in there.

Jack Conway (13)
Hassenbrook GM School

THE COLOUR OF LIGHT

Grey is a mutant colour
It draws vibrant colours
From the very edge of the circle
Inexorably towards the central vortex
And combines them to create
Something new.
Subtly, it hides the brilliance
Or destroys it
To make something new.
In gaining utility
We have lost primacy.

Hidden in white light
With no artifice
Are all the colours.
In case we forget
What we have lost.

Ben Sullivan (13)
Hassenbrook GM School

THE WORLD

Look at the sky so peaceful, so tranquil
Then look at the world you live in
Knowing somewhere else there are children crying.

How can I forget that someone else's life is inhumane
And there is nothing I can do?
People don't tell me about events, instead they keep them hidden.

They think I don't know, too young to understand
But I know what happened
It affects us though it is in a different land
Brothers burning in the sky

But why?

In this land there is so much pain
Wars, fighting, death
But what for? Are we insane?
Can't we be a whole picture instead of pieces of a jigsaw?

We try our best for those in need
But does it make a difference?
I am young, a new seed
Perhaps I can make a difference in this dark land

Look at the world, then look at the sky.

Gary Shilling (13)
Hassenbrook GM School

WAR

The wispy wind and the smoky air,
The pictures of loved ones scattered everywhere.
The firemen and ambulances racing to and fro.
The air raid alarms buzzing everywhere.
Soldiers fighting here and there.

Mum serving the country,
Dad probably dead somewhere.
My brother and sister nowhere to be seen,
All I can hear is shouts and screams,
My ears buzzing like a buzzing bee.

Lisa Kemp (13)
Honywood School

WINTER NIGHT FOOTBALL

The cold air hits you,
As you step our the car,
No matter how many layers you have on,
It still makes your lips blue.

You walk down the road, the stadium in sight,
People in their shirts predicting.

As we arrive at the stadium, wrapped up
Policemen and stewards protecting the ground,
As we buy our programme.

In the ground people sipping tea and eating burgers,
The announcer handing the sponsors signed stuff,
While players are warming up.

Slowly, the players disappear,
As they go and get ready for the match,
The buzzer goes and the players run out
To the cheers and claps from the cold crowd.

The referee flicks a coin,
The team takes centre and it's the whistle
Everyone wants to hear,
It's kick off!

Charlotte Finch (12)
Honywood School

MONEY

You have a lot of money,
So what does that mean?
Will you get a better place in heaven,
Or a ringside seat in life?
No, I think it means
You have a lot of money.
I think you hold metal in your fist
And it seems metal has clamped your brain!
Money does your talking for you,
Money props your eyes open,
See, you are even too lazy
To clothe and feed yourself.
Money will do it all for you.

You have a lot of metal and paper,
What a splendid clatter it makes!
Look how the coins shine and glitter,
But what it is worth?

So you have money,
You will spend it on food fit for kings,
But who will be better off
You or your vendor?
Now you hold food
And no shiny money fills your wallet.
What a pity you didn't listen
When I explained it all before,
Then it wouldn't be such a shock.

The money which holds open your eyes
One day will slip
And you will not know
How to open them again.

Money doesn't answer to you anymore,
You will be left in the dark,
So at least learn
How to open your eyes
Before you write another cheque.

Jean White (13)
Honywood School

SCARED STIFF!

As I walk across the lonely street, bombs flying overhead,
How I wish I could be in my cosy bed.

One foot in front of the other, wondering if this
Would be my last step.

Wanting to run home, but scared stiff with fear,
Mum and Dad told me that I would be better off here.

When I stumbled onto the wooden train,
There were at least 100 other children crying for their mums,
As I turned around staring at the injured with their gunshot
Arms and sore fingers and thumbs.

The train started moving to a faraway place,
If you look around you see nothing but children
With tears running down their faces.

They all look so lonely, so sad and so scared,
If only the people who were dropping the bombs cared.

As the trains move further away from our homes,
All that you could hear was the wounded soldiers and
Their painful moans.

With name tags and gas masks, we were on the way
With apprehension and fear of tomorrow, a new day.

Rebecca Yexley (12)
Honywood School

GETTING MY NEW BIKE

Something I really liked,
Was getting my new bike,
We started out early,
We visited the shop,
We struck a bargain
And got a free bottle of pop.

It's a blue mountain tamer,
Without a mountain to tame,
Front and back suspension
To calm the humps and bumps,
Not designed for mega jumps,
To use the 18 gears,
Would bring anyone to tears.

We put it together,
Which took forever,
I got my dad to help,
By gosh he ain't half clever,
We then went for a ride,
I came back with a sore backside.

Matthew Roberts (11)
Honywood School

DINOSAURS

The world was dark and dangerous
When dinosaurs roamed about
These creatures were fantastic
Of that there is no doubt.

Some dinosaurs were long
Some dinosaurs were tall
Some of them could swim
And some of them could crawl.

Some dinosaurs were fierce
They made a sound like moans
It's hard for me to picture it
I've only seen their bones!

Michael Howell (11)
Honywood School

WHY?

Why is the world unfair?
Why can't the world be peaceful?
Why can't we have fair people in this world?
Why do people have to bully others?
Why do we die?
Why must people suffer and others not?
Why? Have they done something wrong?
Why do we have to do things we don't want to?
Is it fair to treat people badly, to laugh at them?
Is it nice to treat them with respect?
Yes it is.
Everyone is equal in this world.
No one should be horrible.
Why can't you give everyone a second chance?
Why make fun of homeless people?
Why can't you play together?
Why can't we all do the same thing?
Because everyone is different.
The way they eat and talk.
We all have our individual self.
There is no one different.
We all are the same, so why ask the questions
That we ask? All we have to do
Is to treat people with respect.
A bit of love for others is the question.

Jennifer Man (13)
Honywood School

The First Storm

Gently blowing summer breeze,
Leaves swinging on their branches,
The wind picks up,
Leaves swinging harder,
Pitter-patter of tiny raindrops can be heard.
Spines shiver as the wind howls like a wolf,
Animals with waterlogged furs are scurrying for shelter,
Birds flee for safety,
Rain constantly beating the ground,
As ferociously as a grizzly bear,
Rain turns to hail,
Wind turns to hurricane,
Everyone is cold,
Wet and miserable.
The crashing of hailstones blocks out all sound
But the howling and wailing of the
Vicious whirling terror.
The storm is growing! Brewing! Boiling!
Until, the hailstones slowly ease off,
The howling and wailing of the wind dies down,
The blowing halts,
Almost gone, until all that is left is a gentle rainfall
Carried on a slow breeze.

From behind the clouds the sun peers out over the
                              storm wrecked land below
And as the brightly shining sun beams through the rain,
Seven beautiful colours form a huge ark in the sky,
Welcoming the world to a fresh new start.

William Pearmain (12)
Honywood School

UNTITLED

All alone on my own no one to love or care for me,
I'm sitting here on the floor, waiting, waiting . . .
Waiting for someone to carry me off,
I start to spit and splutter,
No one can see me, no one can hear me,
I wonder why? What have I done?
Then I start to hear a tap, tap on the window, tap, tap, tap.
Is it the someone I have been longing for,
The person that carries me off to a distant shore,
It's a man, I can see his moustache,
Has he really come to carry me off or is he just another angry bailiff?
Then I hear another knock on the door, what will I do? What will I say?
What if he breaks down the door and sees me sitting there,
He will wonder why I never opened the door,
What should I do? I'm asking you!

Alex Whitelock (12)
Honywood School

HUNGER

Hunger, such a short word, such a big thing,
When you are eating your toast or cereals just think.
What people in Africa are eating right now,
Maybe a leaf or rice in a bowl.
How can a person survive on a leaf?
Just think that person could be dead next week.
When you are eating pizza crumpets and jam
Be grateful you are not eating maggots out of a pan,
So next time when you hide a pea under your knife,
Every little pea could be somebody's life.

Jessica Barham (13)
Honywood School

FEAR

Destruction causes fear,
The reason for war is unclear,
Death, hate, pain,
Can happen when you hear a German plane.

I call it the teatime raid,
And wonder how many lives have been paid,
They die as heroes while we cower,
At the Germans very power.
When I wish I'm warm in my bed,
Squashed in the bunker, I am instead,
Never a wink of sleep I get,
Friends will end up dead, I fret.

And in the morning everything seems alright,
Apart from bombed houses which give me a fright,
Then I go out to collect souvenirs,
When will this war end, I think through tears.

Lyall Horner (12)
Honywood School

LIFE AND DEATH OF WAR

Planes soaring through the clouds,
Tanks moaning on the ground,
Bombs shooting down to earth,
The floor rumbles,
The roar of the cannons,
The choirs of the screams,
The rattle of the guns,
The wailing of the bombs,
The loudness of the noise,
The power of the tears.

Jack Thomas (11)
Honywood School

Fallout

I gave her a shove when she walked past me,
She glared at me from across the classroom.

I was partners with another girl in English,
She told the teacher I was pulling faces at her.

I put a pencil mark across her maths book,
She put a pen line straight through mine.

I played with somebody else at lunchtime,
She ran away and made fun of me.

I poked my tongue out when she wasn't looking,
She tripped me up when I walked past.

I can't remember how the argument started,
I can almost guarantee she can't either.

We hugged, and both said sorry to each other,
I went round her house after school.

Rebecca Clarke (12)
Honywood School

Total Paradise

Golden sand beneath your feet,
Turquoise sea and aqua sky,
Yellow sun and clouds so neat,
The only noise is the sly seagulls
Pecking at some sandwiches.
All that is left is the gently lapping sea on
The shoreline.
Complete silence,
The beach is deserted.

Emma Killick (11)
Honywood School

SHOES AND FEET

High heels,
Trainers,
Sandals two,
One day I will get them too.
Grubby, smelly, sweaty feet,
I have to scrub them every day,
Always ponging out the house,
Even scare away the mouse,
Brand new school shoes,
Squeaky squeak,
Down the corridors,
Every week.
Mucky boots,
Leave dirt trails,
Squash and squelch,
On poor old snails.
High heel platforms,
Make me tall,
I can't walk at all,
So I'd better stay small,
Slinky sandals,
On the beach
Fun and funky,
In the water,
Comfy, cosy slippers too,
Good for cold days,
Good for when you're poorly
And good for when you have the flu.

Chloe Austin (11)
Honywood School

SKYSCRAPER VIEW

Dust floats, then conceals,
Fumes arise, and then settle
The homeless beg and then pray.
Birds don't sing, not even a note,
Smells drift then are sensed.

From a window
A sheet of buildings glisten before you
Like the sea when the sky is blue.
Everything seems lost,
An endless mass of chaos,
But beneath lies life . . .

Foreigners flash cameras vigorously,
Commuters whistle as they walk,
Businessmen scurry
And police cars hurry.
Black cabs and red buses cruise.
Minicabs drive, then demand.
Trains arrive, then replenish,
Horns sound.
Traffic lights change: red, amber and green.
Churches sit, whilst their spires pray,
And statues stand as proud as Punch.

One might say it's panoramic,
One might say it's a country's bruise
But it's just a city, an ordinary city!

Matt James Abbott
Newport Free Grammar School

SENDING OFF THE OVERPOWERED MEN ONE BY ONE

Sending off the overpowered men one by one,
Only to be killed straight under the sun,
Destroying the sun of God's creation
The lives lost with expression of frustration.

Trying to run on a continuous belt of fear,
To hide and cower away without a tear,
The evil and power within each other,
To kill mankind and lose our brothers.

To walk away, a coward's way of life,
But to stop all this worry and endless strife,
Would brighten it all and take the clouds of sin away,
To leave a gleaming sky and a blissful day.

But, alas, the minds of all humanity,
Do not mend this problem with any dignity,
To border up the future of all offspring,
A crime to take away, their peaceful dreaming.

Jodie Clay (14)
Newport Free Grammar School

A WAR POEM

There's just fighting every day,
In every possible murdering way,
Picture of the family stuck in mind,
But peace and quiet is hard to find.
Three thousand bullets in a round,
Here I wish a homeward bound,
With every bullet from this gun,
I wish I could just turn and run,

Holding on for my treasured life,
With feelings in my heart for the beloved wife.
At night I wish for my fantasy,
That this war would end, the soldiers agree.
So many have suffered for the bad,
Children wanting, screaming, 'Dad!'
The women are suffering on their own,
God help me get back to my home sweet home.

Deborah Hibbitt (15)
Newport Free Grammar School

THE SMALL RED FLOWER

Bullets and shells fly overhead,
Hark! Another man falls dead.
He falls for eternity, never resting
The fight continues until our final testing.

Now it is night and we should be asleep,
I hear the creature of the night creep.
A scream, there goes another,
One more to join his brother.

Our lives are gone and so is the light,
The demons are here, here in our fight,
We stand in the mud, mud made of blood,
A shot, a scream, a hell, a thud.

The sigh of death is the only sound,
There's a haze of red, all over the ground
No blood, no fighting, no more power,
Only the eternal scent, of the small red flower.

Nicole Younie (14)
Newport Free Grammar School

THE CITY AND THE COUNTRYSIDE

The city - a place full of pollution, noise and cunning
Beggars, tramps, nurses, nobles, rich and poor,
A place full of hassle, hurrying, rushing and running,
With thieves and robbers, with evil plans of breaking the law.

The countryside - a place of rest and needful peace,
A place of sun and rain and wind and white, white snow,
A place of happiness, animals and lives of carefree ease,
Open and free where the wind can freshly blow and blow.

In the city - an orphan child crouching low, cold and sad,
His face is white from poor food and air,
A little boy, in surroundings so unhealthy and bad,
His face a picture of woe, no loving mother to give him her care.

In the countryside - in the woods, dark and gloomy,
Bluebells scattering a rough, narrow, windy track,
Away from the city, unhealthy and fumey,
The track leading to an old, quaint woodcutter's shack.

In the city, rich people zooming around in expensive motors,
With ladies wearing sparkling, valuable necklaces,
Estate agents, always buzzing around, making quotes
And hundreds of new faces to see, all different faces.

In the countryside - the lark and the nightingale merrily sing,
Where deer roam and black and white badgers romp
And that quaint legend of old, or mushrooms all in a ring
And the fresh pastures, grazing grounds for cows to stomp!

The city and the countryside, an opposite so vast,
The countryside - badgers, deer, rabbits and trees,
The city - beggars, sickness and cars whizzing by, fast,
The city and the countryside, fumes, illness, lambs and
A fresh cool breeze!

Natalie Christie (12)
Newport Free Grammar School

FOXES

We are foxes,
Watching the darkness Hitler has created,
Waiting in the burrow of bloodied earth,
We hear them.

While the moon watched in disbelief,
We waited and heard them approaching like dark
                              whispers on the wind,
We saw their tired white faces,
We waited still as a pool of water glistening in the night's light,
Would we be seen?
'Whoosh!' the bullets hummed past my head.

I sat stunned,
In horror I saw in the corner of my eye,
Inching towards me was my friend's blood.
One of the bullets had shot him in the head,
I couldn't wipe my splattered face,
I could be seen.

So I sat,
Silent,
Still,
Shell-shocked,
Next to my dead best friend.

I am a *fox*
Watching the darkness that Hitler has created.

Natalie Howlett (14)
Newport Free Grammar School

TOGETHER

We were family and always together,
Playing games with each other
And always loving for ever and ever,
Mother, father, wife and brother,
We stuck together through thick and thin
And never, ever gave up loving.

We were brothers larking around,
Going along with the game,
Believing we were safe and sound
And never feeling any shame,
Then came the news we were waiting for,
The time had come, we were off to war.

We were soldiers playing the game,
Fighting for ourselves
And for our country's name,
The firing of bullets and dropping of shells,
The time had come
And we had nowhere to run.

We were broken, our families gone,
Nothing to fight for,
Because the war was won,
We love no more,
But we still go on,
Living in heaven, as the war is won.

Simon Wilks (14)
Newport Free Grammar School

THE WINGS OF A FALLEN ANGEL

The way a man laughs as he dies,
The way a mother smiles as she gets the telegram,
The way a son plays as mother shares the news,
The way a family rejoice when father never returns,
That is the wing of a fallen angel.

The way a town mourns the end of fighting,
The way a world is heartsick as peace comes,
The way a city cries when the calm descends,
The tears on a safe man's face,
That is the wing of a fallen angel.

The smile of a baby's burning flesh,
The sweet scent of disease,
The giggle of a tortured man,
The fine view of cascading blood,
That is the wing of a fallen angel.

The horror on the face of a free man,
The hatred in the eye of a newborn baby,
The rage of a child at play,
How we envy the incapacitated man,
That is the wing of a fallen angel.

These are the wings of a fallen angel,
The wings of a fallen angel,
What is left when the wings are gone?

Marshall Hulance (14)
Newport Free Grammar School

My War Poem

As he walked away with joy in his heart,
The time had come for him to play his part,
As he put the gun in his palms,
I wished for him in my arms.

As I look at young children play-fighting,
He is facing real pain at the speed of lightning,
As I am surrounded in warmth by my family
I can only think of him so lonely.

As he stays awake in the long, dark night,
Dreading the break of the glaring sunlight,
As he lies in terror so quiet and still,
The other side are coming, ready to kill.

As I rush to the door and look through the mail,
My heart beats faster, I start to feel ill and pale,
As I look, I notice, I have no replies,
I only hope he has run out of supplies.

Gemma Perman (14)
Newport Free Grammar School

Soldiers

Soldiers march away to war
Full of excitement and adventure,
From the crowd there came a roar
As fathers, sons and husbands left,
Many of them never to be seen again.

None knew of the terror they
Would have to face on the battlefield,
Not once did anyone say
That war was anything but glorious,
No fear was felt from those men that day.

All their dreams came crashing down,
When they saw the hell surrounding them,
The sound of gunfire all around,
Dead men lying everywhere,
It was the grave of thousands.

None of the soldiers felt brave anymore.

Eilidh Torbett (14)
Newport Free Grammar School

WAR LIFE

We sit in our trenches,
In the middle of a war,
With stains and stenches,
We sit on the floor.

As shells fly overhead,
We sit and dream,
Of our warm cosy bed,
Oh, how good they can seem.

I think of my children,
My parents and wife,
Back home in London,
Would be the life.

As a bomb drops nearby,
I suddenly awake,
I jump up high
And a deep breath I take.

Out of my trench I hop,
My bayonet poised
I went over the top
And joined the boys.

Ben Williams (14)
Newport Free Grammar School

THE TRENCHES

Eight days I've gone without a wash,
My clothes once green, now a dirty brown,
We sit and talk of the things we miss,
No jokes, no laughs, our faces frown.

As rats run around our aching feet,
We sit and chew on stale old bread,
We bend down suddenly, crouching low
A shell is screeching overhead.

All day, all night, you hear screams and cries,
Another bomb exploding nearby,
Noises nobody wants to hear
Then eerie silence as someone else dies.

We came with dreams of action and fun,
As heroes we would all go home,
But our blood washes the fields in the setting sun,
And we are left scared and alone.

Clare McPartland (14)
Newport Free Grammar School

ONE WAY TICKET

We watched the men marching off one by one,
Helmets attached to their heads,
Peering at them until they are gone,
Knowing if not returned, they are dead.

During the evening I'll be on my own,
The children will have gone to sleep,
Sitting, reading my book all alone,
The love in my heart for him weeps.

Now our farewells have been told,
There is no *coming back*,
He will sit there in the freezing cold,
Looking at his only possessions in the old,
Brown pack.

Helena Bland (14)
Newport Free Grammar School

THE PRICE WE HAVE TO PAY

Our way of life has been threatened
And we must answer the call.
It's not up to a handful of people
Protecting freedom will take us all.

The price of freedom has always been high
But can't be measured by the pounds it cost,
Or can a value ever be placed
On lives that have or will be lost.

I'm not only talking about our soldiers
Who took a job defending our land,
I'm also talking of the innocent,
The targets of an evil plan.

So will it be our mothers and fathers
Or daughters or our sons?
How many lives must be put on the line
Before this war is won?

But it's been that way throughout history
And it's the high price we have to pay,
The best thing to do now is not worry
Just bow your head and pray.

Laura Forman (14)
Newport Free Grammar School

SAYING GOODBYE

I packed my bags the night before
And left them by the door,
That night I didn't sleep a wink,
All I did was have a think.

I thought of all the good times
In the past and knowing that
Memories will always last.

I tell my kids I'll be back soon
But deep down knowing
It won't be that soon.

And when I arrived at the army base,
I steeled myself and put on a brave face.

Soon after that we were sent to war,
Not watching the football, not knowing the score.
Not like in the movies not anymore.

Felicity Fairweather (14)
Newport Free Grammar School

WE'RE GOING OFF TO WAR!

We're going off to war!
It's what we've waited for,
Living in a trench, hungry, tired and cold,
We probably won't live until we're very old.
If we make any friends in this awful place
They will be dead in a few days
We want to go home, we wish we'd never come.
We're thinking of food, how we wish for some.

We hear the sound of people dying
Mixed with all the brave men crying.
We hear the screams of bullets flying
Then the men alive are sighing.
It will only be a matter of time
Until we're killed on the front line.
We're off to war!
It's what we've waited for.

Sarah Peak (14)
Newport Free Grammar School

THE PRESS RELEASE

You'll get rich for the price of one soul
But you won't be in control, others dictate your goals
Your opinions over all, your being they'll have dominion
66.6 FM is the frequency they read on
Radio controllers, record companies that make stacks
As they distort facts then press it on wax
You see it, African accents masked by John Bull or Uncle Sam
You claim there was emancipation but Bush lies to the common man
Why is it that you must live up to a person's ideology?
And why do crooked men become the subject of idolatry?
I'll tell you why! The media is controlled by crooked men
He who pays the piper calls the tune let's not pretend
No dividends, are paid to people who uphold the upper classes
It's all around you but you wear New Labour's rose tinted glasses
The propaganda 'Great'Britain what a joke
It's enough to make me choke, the media's rope
Now has a hold over the culture, which I express
I digress that this one-sided system is a mess
Where's my press? These aren't my words!
This is what suffocates me
Perceptions propagated by press poison our society.

Kayombo Chingonyi (15)
Robert Clack Comprehensive Upper School

DON'T DO DRUGS

A high and a spin, a rush and a grin,
Give me another one, it's really working,
All problems are gone, worries forgotten,
A headache and a stomach ache,
Back breaking pain,
Sick, sick, down the drain, body unconscious,
Lying on the floor,
The best friend I had is here no more.

Candice H White (13)
Sir Charles Lucas Arts College, Colchester

THE UNLUCKY ROUND

Early in the morning you may view,
A cyclist's lights illuminating the dew,
As he heads off on his round,
He picks up his load
And starts delivering down the road,
He came to his favourite part,
A huge hill that he can zoom down,
The hill goes slightly round,
Halfway down his foot hits the tarmac,
For a moment he was unstable,
He recovered and then hit a bottle,
His bike flew through the air and then hit the kerb,
He ends up
Not quite sure what way up,
In a thorn bush,
He gets up off the ground
And continues with the round,
He forgot a house and so goes back,
He rode home unhappy,
This unlucky person was me.

Jonathan Caumont (13)
St Helena School, Colchester

MY WORLD, OUR WORLD

Our world, this planet,
What a beautiful place,
I'll tell you all the things,
That put a smile on my face.

> The sea, the sea,
> A long ribbon of blue,
> That winks at me
> And smiles at you.

The sand, the sand,
A fine desert of gold,
Soft to the hand
And hard to hold.

> Mountains and lakes,
> Can be wherever,
> Like icing on cakes,
> Always together.

Insects and fish,
Reptiles and mammals,
It is my wish,
To save all these animals.

> Butterflies and birds,
> Always on duty,
> Not enough words,
> To explain their beauty.

Peace, peace,
That comes with a dove,
May it never cease
And let there be love.

Roxana Kashani (14)
St Helena School, Colchester

AFTERMATH OF WAR

Deserted,
This world has nothing left.
Everything has been destroyed,
Nothing remains standing.

Depression,
There's people wandering the streets,
Crying out for their loved ones,
As they were lost in the battle.

Dismal,
The sky is grey and gloomy,
No buildings are standing,
There are only remains.

Deafening,
The pain in the cries are like glass in your ears,
Calling out for comfort and love,
Just wanting to be whole again.

Destruction,
This is what our world has become,
A battleground for all,
War has destroyed our world.

Naomi Pike (13)
St Helena School, Colchester

NIGHT-TIME

Shadows creeping up the wall,
Some are very, very tall!
The moon stays awake all through the night,
Watching over the children, tucked up tight!

The night-time sky starts departing
And another day is starting!
Night-time will visit us again tomorrow
And every day the same will follow!

Alice Polley (12)
St Helena School, Colchester

MY KINGDOM

In my room, I lie on my bed,
I close my eyes and think.

I float up high, above the clouds,
Twisting, turning, soaring the sky.

I see people down below me,
Their eyes mesmerised,
As they bow down to me,
As I gently land near a castle.

My kingdom, peace at last,
No wars, no fears,
The sun to shine,
The moon to glow,
A tranquil place full of harmony.

I open my eyes,
I view a screen,
War for all to see,
To last forever,
For all eternity.

Emma Harrigan (13)
St Helena School, Colchester

DREAMS

Dreams, they float in and out of being,
Bringing us joy, filling us with sorrow,
What do they look like?
Does no one know?
Are they shimmering clouds of colour,
Or invisible foe?
What shall we dream?
We cannot tell,
Will it haunt or relieve us?
Does no one know?
With this power our mind endlessly battles,
Not willing to give in,
To lose this fight.
Dreams always win; and, as they fill our thoughts,
Our mind watches, the loser again.
The dream comes to an end,
Our mind has control
It vows never to be defeated again.
Dreams, they float in and out of being,
Bringing us joy, filling us with sorrow.

Verity Grimsey (14)
St Helena School, Colchester

THE LION

In the forests of the night,
His big, black eyes stare beady and bright,
His sharp, white teeth glisten and glow,
He is slinking around, lying low,
He's searching for dinner, he's on the prowl,
He spots his prey and lets out a growl,
The fierce predator leaps off his feet,
The power of the animal is extremely elite,

Through the long strands of grass,
He rustles silently past,
His razor teeth sparkle and then pierce through the skin,
Of his innocent victim bleeding within,
Secondly the claws appear
And stab through the heart of the poor young deer.

Sarah Halls (13)
St Helena School, Colchester

PRISON REGRETS

Rotting away in this tiny cell,
Thinking, *surely I'll go to Hell.*
I'm regretting what I did last night,
I've already been in a fight,
I'm feeling cold and lonely now,
Trying to work out why, and how?
Iron bars let in a little light,
Scared and guilty I sleep at night.
Tossing and turning in my bed,
Horror movies running through my head.
I wonder what tomorrow will be like?
Will it be another fight?
Living like this in a lot of pain,
Longing for freedom once again.
Will I ever rid of this nightmare?
Thinking, surely this isn't fair.
I'll die all lonely in this place,
Never to see a familiar face,
It's all my fault, I've done it now,
Wishing I hadn't, wondering how?

Laura Price (12)
St Helena School, Colchester

THE LAND OF DREAMS AND MAKE BELIEVE

The dusty, yellow, sparkling new sand,
Lay on the deserted beach,
Being swept up by the deep blue sea,
Into a land of dreams and make believe.

Where the fishes glittered and sparkled like a living disco ball,
Flashing at the dancers below,
The seaweed swaying in the flow of the sea like a Mexican wave,
The dancing lobsters jigged about all night long,
Rocking the dance floor,
The band playing all kinds of music,
With their shell saxophones and coral guitars.

But all this was distorted by a small green fishing boat,
Chugging along no sense of all the havoc below,
Everyone runs for their lives
As the long, shiny hook dangles in the untouched sea,
Tempting a creature with its meaty surprise.

And up he comes to the real world, dazed and confused,
Looking up at the happy fisherman,
'I have caught one' he cried 'I will eat you for my tea.'

As he left fracturing the land of dreams and make believe,
Ripping the deep blue sea,
Creaking the deserted beach
And untidying the dusty yellow sparkling new sand,
Not thinking of the beautiful land he had broken.

Amy Robinson (13)
St Helena School, Colchester

CANCER

Cancer starts from the first to the last,
It spreads like a cold inside of you,
You're filled with pain, anger and hurt,
You try to sleep, but your head's filled with unhappiness.

You try to work, but you're too weak to stay,
You know it's there, there's nothing you can do,
You want to turn back time, to the beginning,
Change your whole life.

Your family and friends are worried and scared,
You want to help but there's nothing you can do,
The worst is never over
And how did it start?
From their first to their last.

Danielle Cheasley (13)
St Helena School, Colchester

DREAMS

Dreams are the best place to be,
They astound and confuse me.
Nightmares are scary and frightening,
But a real nice dream is very enlightening.

In my dream I'm in a fantasy place,
In my dream I could see anyone's face,
In my dream I can be rich and in love,
In my dream I could be floating above.

In my dream I could be at the seaside,
In my dream I could be watching the rough tide,
In my dream I could be in the Amazon,
Looking at the sky that's crimson.

Ashleigh Martinez (13)
St Helena School, Colchester

INFLICTION

I slashed my wrist giving the knife a final twist
Why can't I find that inner peace?
I have to get a form of release
A way to ease the suffering you're causing me
Letting the blood pour from my view
To try and release the pain
You may call it self-abuse
Or maybe you think I use it as an attention seeking excuse
I have to avoid facing up to my harsh reality
I can't help it, it's my mentality
I confess to you that I prefer self-denial
That's the easy option.
Every scar becomes a memory
Too painful for me to forget
Scar tissue holding my wounds together
Holding me together
Keeping me in the life
I've now got to hate
Waiting for that soul to save my own
Before it is sent to the fiery depths of Hell
And sent into damnation for all eternity.
Are you my knight who saves my abused soul?
Take me
Teach me
Hate me
Love me.

Julianne Carter (17)
South East Essex Sixth Form College

WAKE

The room filled up quickly after the church,
Their faces clouded by sadness,
You wouldn't believe it was a party,
Her mother was crying into her brandy,
Her father was denying her death,
I was dying inside,
It was a celebration of her life,
Of her death,
Of my dying.

Lisa Winsor (17)
South East Essex Sixth Form College

AN UNKNOWN PLACE, AN UNKNOWN FIGURE

The skeletal claw dug deep in my skin
Was it a punishment for committing a sin?
I was pulled out of bed to an unknown place
Seeing my ugly, scabbed kidnapper's face,
I was dragged and hauled, until let go
The feeling of terror was strong, oh no!
His body was hidden by a ragged black cloak
His hand lowered to my neck - was I to choke?
His grip tightened, I panted, I wheezed,
Hit hot foul breath on my face caused a breeze,
I closed my eyes, so tight I felt pain
But when I felt nothing, opened them again,
I was no longer troubled, safe and warm,
Secure at home, awake in my dorm.

Michaela Dunn (13)
The Plume School

NIGHTMARE

Oh it was terrifying
And it was petrifying.

It made me shocked
And it made me scared.

It was dark
And I heard a dog bark.

Then I saw a bear
With long, straggly hair.

Then he opened his mouth
And I saw something in the south.

I moved closer in
And I saw a piece of human skin.

I suddenly froze to a stop
His tongue was moving like a clock.

Tick-tock, tick-tock.

I turned to run away from the beast
But failed to escape to the east.

It stretched its hand and grabbed me
He was holding me by the knee.

He opened his mouth
And I knew I was gonna end at the south.

He took me in, I felt him bite
Then I knew I couldn't fight,
I couldn't fight.

I was dead and there was no turning back!
I felt as if I were in a sack!

Tammy Wright (13)
The Plume School

THE END

During the time in which your mind falls asleep
While you twist and you turn
And your eyeballs burn,
You belong to the Nightmare Prince.

Falling and falling, faster and faster,
Chocking in pain trying to stop
Inevitably you drop,
You belong to the Nightmare Prince.

Once you hit the ground,
You're immersed in salt water,
Hearing the screams of the previously slaughtered,
You belong to the Nightmare Prince.

Trying to breathe to swim to the top,
In the distance you see a warm glowing light,
Will you give up your fight?
You belong to the Nightmare Prince.

The screaming gets louder,
Your head starts to hurt,
Until you land on the cold, hard dirt
You belong to the Nightmare Prince.

When you open your eyes,
The screaming has stopped, after your long, hard drop,
Are you awake now?
You belong to the Nightmare Prince.

Chris Herber (13)
The Plume School

THE END

I lay still in bed
I close my eyes
The sun is shining
People are talking
The birds are screeching
The sky is blue
Cars are zooming
Babies are crying
The sun is smiling
Smiles are smiling
People are walking
The sun is still shining.

I am walking to another world
Crossing the bridge of life or death
Cars are still zooming
I open my eyes to look
The sun is still shining
Bang!

The blue sky turns to black
The sun turns to a moon
The birds are not screeching
Cars are not zooming
Babies are not crying
Silence!
Peace!

> Smiles are not smiling
> It's the end for me
> It's the end of the world
> But everyone is still living
> I am gone forever
> The sun is not shining
> It's the end for me.

Lianna Cudby (14)
The Plume School

SKELETONS OF SNOW

S keletons of snow
K nifes embedded deeply in the soft white carpet
E vening ends and night begins
L aughter creeps through the spinney forest
E choes travel through the night
T rees swaying like dancing bones
O ut there I know I'm not alone
N ewly made footprints, fresh in the snow
S keletons of snow.

O ver the treetops the owls hunt
F rightened prey and me.

S hadowy figures haunt around me
N erves creek down my spine
O ver my shoulder I look to find . . .
W aken I do!

Christopher Johnson (14)
The Plume School

NIGHTMARE POEM

It's dark, it's gloomy and the sky is velvet-blue
And I'm totally unaware about what to do . . .
Should I run and carry on
Or is this walkway just a con?
I can't see the end
Or a forthcoming bend
But I hope and believe
And soon comes relief
For soon I see an awaited turn
And my destiny I shall soon learn!
I take the turn, walk then run
But still there is no sign of the sun.
I'm shocked and scared at what I see
As I stare, I ask myself, how could this be?
Five old hags watch and stare,
Then they all give me an evil glare.
No colour in their eyes and their hair is grey,
They point to a bed and tell me to lay
Scared and unsure, I decide to trust
Then my worry turns to lust
As they read my destiny, I see a man
But I soon realise there's a restricted ban
As I realise it's fantasy, just pure illusion
I feel my destiny foretell intrusion.
My feelings are banished, stomped away
The rest of my soul died that day
As I turned around I saw him still
What was his intention, to want to kill?
The hags were laughing and blue in the face
My dreams had been mocked and fully disgraced
For as they told the final part of my destiny
I realised this love just wasn't to be
For as I looked at this man once again.

My life and dreams began to wane
For he was evil, Saturn's work,
As a knife out of his pocket started to lurk
He took the knife and stabbed my back
And my heartbeat soon began to lack . . .
For soon all I saw in my mind was blood
A gushing waterfall turning into a flood
But then I awoke from my nightmare dream
And realised that some things just aren't what they seem!

Hanane Yahiaoui
The Plume School

NIGHTMARE

I fell asleep under the moon expecting to wake soon,
Deep in my slumber, I could hear loud banging thunder
And the day looked like noon.

My bed flying high, spinning round in the sky,
Birds flying past and from the thunder came a blast,
It showed a mysterious guy.

Anxiously looking around me, but nothing did I see,
Where was I? And how did I fly?
The mysterious face began sniggering with glee.

My body shook in fear, as I spotted the face coming near,
I could hear someone sing and the sound of
'Bling . . . bling . . . bling!'
Then my heartbeat increased its pace.

I closed my eyes so tight, thinking it was still night,
With the sunlight piercing through, it was then that I knew,
It was all a terrible fright!

Charlotte Bacon (13)
The Plume School

Running Scared

I am running as fast as I can,
Through the dark wood,
My face burning like fire,
My legs aching.

I hear voices from behind me,
Her footprints,
I hear them yell,
Her footprints.

I need to stop,
I have to stop,
I can't stop,
They will hunt me down like dogs.

I try to speed up,
I fall,
I look down at my hands,
Blood,
Covered in blood.

I jump to my feet,
I can hear them,
They are coming closer,
I hear their hungry voices.

My heart pounding,
My body shaking,
I am terrified.

I hear a piercing scream,
I realise it was me,
I feel a stabbing pain,
There are people around me,
My heart beating fast,
I wake.

Sophie Mardon (13)
The Plume School

NIGHTMARE

I'm falling through darkness,
The wind's breath is cold and harsh,
The darkness spreads,
I see my friends in the distance,
They cannot hear me!

Sadness sweeps through me,
The light slowly fades,
Like a candle left in the wind
The ground is nearer,
The sea twinkles in the moonlight.

I fall forward,
Nearer and nearer the sea,
The sea's mouth opens to welcome me,
I keep falling . . . is this the end?

Hayley Bond (13)
The Plume School

THE CHASE IN THE JUNGLE

Out in the dark, on my own, I'm afraid
Rustles and bustles around me
Down on the ground on grass which I laid
The roar of the waves from the sea.

A crunch to my left of a twig or a stick
Warns me that something is near
My eyes are whizzing as my head starts to tick
And my ears prick up as to hear.

I clamber to my feet and start to run
While images zoom round in my head
Why is it chasing me, this terrible scum?
Please chase something else instead.

Through leaves, flowers, bushes and branches
As moisture dampens my clothes
Climbing through gaps and taking my chances
Suddenly an opening shows.

My foot gets caught in the root of a tree
And my body falls flat to the ground
I squirm on the floor to try and see
The owner of the sickening sound.

A rotting smell reaches my nose
A warm breeze of air on my neck
Saliva drips on my cheek as it shows
I can't bring myself to check.

I finally turned my head around
To see the creature beside me
I expected the animal to make a sound,
But just stared at me queerly.

Its fiery red eyes pierced my lungs
And its large pointed teeth glistened
Saliva dripped from its huge lolling tongue,
As I lay on the floor imprisoned.

I can't die like this, waiting for death!
I had to try, to do my best
My strength returned and I held my breath
And kicked the great beast in the chest.

I climbed to my feet and ran ahead
Where the opening lay just beyond me
Hoping that the monster was dead,
I appeared by a clearing and whooped with glee.

Alexandra Howat (13)
The Plume School

NIGHTMARE

I landed with a start, in the forest, in the dark,
Getting up from the shadowed ground and taking
A moment to look around,
Drawing a breath inside, my first reaction is to run!
To hide! The air around me dark and cold!
I begin to feel brave and bold.
My actions were delayed, I could not think.
My nerves were frayed.
There was something there. I could feel.
Whatever it was, it must have been real.
As much as I had tried and dared,
I still awoke afraid and scared.

Sarah Wynn (13)
The Plume School

MY NIGHTMARE

It was a very dark night
I had a terrible fright,
I was the only person at home.

All of a sudden a storm brewed,
I thought this can't be true,
Because the rain had been falling all day.

The lights flickered, then went off,
I jumped when I glimpsed a moth,
I already had chills down my spine.

I saw a white light in the bedroom,
It looked weird in such a gloom,
So I slowly edged towards the door.

The door slowly crept open,
The sight I saw was choking,
I felt sick in such a horror.

There laid a man, his wounds looked like cud
And the floor was covered in his blood,
The terror slowly arose within me.

Then I awoke,
From a sharp poke,
Which was sent from our younger brother.

Daniel South (13)
The Plume School

DEATH FROM SCHOOL

On a cold shuddery night,
In a dream of such fright
A little girl I am at school.

Silence is around us
No one making any fuss
In the school grounds everyone waits.

The school bells ring,
Children shout with such sin
As we pile through the cold glass doors.

People yelling at me
Like the man on TV
The Jerry Springer show starts to begin.

Running so fast
Down a road so vast
Children bolting after me like thunder.

Through the deep, dark wood
Where an old man once stood
Doesn't stand there anymore.

Running footsteps no more
When I fall to the floor
Down the deep, dark hole of death.

Emma Pollard (13)
The Plume School

THAT NIGHT

I had just closed my eyes and started to sleep
Little did I know it would be far from fun
It crept in whilst in a very deep sleep
The nightmare had come and there was nowhere to run.

Looking around, no way out could be found
There were many people but none looked at me
Far away was my house - I turned around
To reach my family but they couldn't see me.

My family seemed gone forever
And all that I'd have was people who didn't care,
But suddenly a knife seemed to sever
Sleep from wake, and forced me from its lair.

Tim Wade (13)
The Plume School

NIGHTMARE

N ight-time you fear, for death is near,
I n your warm bed, thoughts run through your head,
G o to terrible places, see familiar faces,
H ide from your fright, through the pounding night,
T ry to break away, but you can just stare in dismay,
M onsters surround me, why would they want me?
A round and around, silence! There isn't a sound,
R eality hits home, I know I'm not alone,
E xit is near, nothing left to fear.

James Byrom (13)
The Plume School

THE DEMON

I toss and turn in my nice cosy bed
Thinking of the day including my ted,
I fall into a black hole made of my bin
And I taste the sweet smell of the sin,
I fall into my car
And drink in a bar
The days of my sin
That I put in my bin
A caped man runs into the street above,
I fly like a dove
I feel like a bird happy,
The man jumps out after feeling quite sappy
I fall down and kill the ones I love
I no longer feel like a dove,
The one who killed them was the monster
That killed them including my soul,
It was me the monster I've become now
After I do the crime I do a little bow,
The demon in me is not real
As much as my next full meal
The demon is me
There is no we
Just little old me,
Time slowly passes the street
I feel like a piece of meat
My soul has gone
Stolen!
By that big scary demon.

Amy Baker (13)
The Plume School

THE CHANGING WEATHER

Winter,
One cold winter's day,
I'm going outside to play,
Now I'm going home.

Spring,
It is boiling hot,
Nature is out to play now,
It is really hot.

Summer,
Summer is not hot,
Oh is that a spot?
Come on in and play.

Autumn,
Leaves are falling off,
It is quite warm today out,
I've got a big coat.

Daniel O'Sullivan (11)
Thomas Lord Audley & Language College

HAIKU

It is really cold
I'm glad I've got a fire
It is still snowing.

Lots of daffodils
In the sky there's lots of sun
Even though it's cold.

I have caught the sun
The sun has got his hat on
Hip hip hip hooray!

Why can't it be warm?
Leaves are falling off the trees,
I have a huge coat.

Georgina Pacey (11)
Thomas Lord Audley & Language College

I CAN SEE

I can see children
Playing in the park.

I have seen them playing,
Hide and seek in the dark.

In my car I can see
Someone trying to find their keys.

There are many things,
Moving in the trees.

Little babies crawling
On their knees.

The journey's coming to a stop,
There are so many things and
That's the lot.

Toni Peperell (11)
Thomas Lord Audley & Language College

HAIKU SEASONS

Winter
On a winter's day
Santa Claus brings us presents
The fire is burning.

Spring
Spring is very nice
All the lovely rabbits play
In the fields all day.

Summer
I am really hot
Hotter than the boiling sun
Everyone will melt.

Autumn
Everyone is gone
All the green leaves are dying
Falling to the ground.

Amy Birch (11)
Thomas Lord Audley & Language College

HAIKU SCHOOL POEM

When I'm doing maths,
All you do is add up sums,
It is so boring.

In school I get bored,
When I'm doing boring work,
I end up snoring!

When I do PE,
I get really exhausted
And I do not care.

When I do rugby,
I take people off their feet,
Although I am small.

Mark Wynne (12)
Thomas Lord Audley & Language College

HAIKU, HAIKU ALL ABOUT FOOD

Bananas are green,
Peanuts and banana rolls,
They are so yummy.

Olives are horrid,
They are round and they are yuck,
They are green and black.

I like all these things,
Oreos dipped in butter
It is so yummy.

Bananas are best,
I have a thing about them
They will rule the world!

Rachel Barnett (11)
Thomas Lord Audley & Language College

MY FAVOURITE SEASONS

Winter
On a winter's day
Snow is very, very cold,
You will need gloves.

Spring
On a spring day
A new baby boy is born
It's really fun.

Summer
On a summer's day
Hotter than all the children
Everything will melt.

Autumn
On an autumn day
The leaves are changing to red,
Like my lovely bed.

Stacey Reubins (11)
Thomas Lord Audley & Language College

MY SEASON HAIKU POEM

In winter it's cold,
So wrap up tight by your mum
And have some cocoa.

In spring baby's come
The birds start to chirp and chirp
The animals walk.

Autumn the leaves fall,
They are lovely and yellow,
It rains all day long.

In summer it's hot,
We have water fights - it's fun
We get very wet.

Rebecca Emily Mary Readman (11)
Thomas Lord Audley & Language College

FOOD

Chocolate is yummy,
It is soft and very smooth,
I like it a lot.

Cheese and tomatoes,
Is a popular flavour,
For eating pizza.

Ice cream is sloppy,
It comes in many flavours,
It is very cold.

I like oven chips,
With Heinz red tomato sauce,
I always eat them.

Teshawna Fisher (12)
Thomas Lord Audley & Language College

LITTLE THINGS

Tight, blue, denim jeans,
Snazzy high golden shoes,
Pretty make-up free.

Fluffy cats and dogs,
Chirpy chicks pecking at corn,
Fishy swims away.

Little boys and girls
Get bullied by big boys and girls,
So they hide away.

Big waves splash by us
Little waves come up the shore
The great typhoon dies.

Lucy Beaumont (11)
Thomas Lord Audley & Language College

COUNTRY SOUNDS

The tip-tapping of the silent rain falling in the pond,
The crunch of people walking through the jewelled grass,
The sound of the birds singing in the early morn,
The squeak of the swing in a secret garden,
The swoshing of the water at the end of the waterfall,
The whistle of the wind blowing through the trees,
The buzz of the bee pollinating the flowers.

Amanda Rand (11)
Thomas Lord Audley & Language College

SEASONS HAIKU

Winter is quite cold
Snowballs are all around us
Snow falls to the ground
Leaves fall from the trees,
Rabbits bouncing and jumping,
But it is not cold,
Summer is quite hot,
I do not wear a T-shirt,
I go to the sea,
Chicks are being born,
Small babies awake and yawn,
Cocoons open wide.

Peter Franklin (11)
Thomas Lord Audley & Language College

ALLITERATION POEM

Angry Amy ate apricots,
Gorgeous Georgina grins greatly,
Sensible Shawna smells sweetly
Tough Toni talks tarty,
Dancer Deanne, deadly, daring,
Lifeless Liam loves Lacy,
Sporty Steven smells sick,
Ally Alex ate apples,
Loopy Lucy loves Liam,
Happy Howkins howls horribly,
Sexy Stacey smiles sweetly.

Leighann Davison (11)
Thomas Lord Audley & Language College

My City Rhyme

We looked on the floor and we saw litter,
We drove past a pub and we saw people drinking bitter,
There was a person on a bicycle,
There was a baby on a tricycle,
Then we drove past a field with lots of tall trees,
We look in the trees and saw honeypots and bees,
We've been driving for ages on the road,
We drove past a pond with a great big toad,
We got out our car and stroked a dog,
My brother Peter took an hour catching a frog.

Steven Barrett (11)
Thomas Lord Audley & Language College

My Journey

I was on my way to the shops,
I wanted a pair of socks,
The teacher was very mad,
The children were very sad,
TLA is the best,
Better than all the rest,
The thing I hate most is homework,
The thing I like most is French,
Everybody at lunchtime lurks
And at break time people sit on benches.

Deanne MacDonald (12)
Thomas Lord Audley & Language College

My Journey

On my trip I saw some trees,
I saw a dog and it had fleas,
In a field there were some cows,
In the barn, there was a mouse.
In a town there were lots of people
And a church with a tall steeple,
I saw the sky it was white
And a plane and a kite,
I saw four sheep,
They were asleep,
There were cows mooing
And pigs chewing,
There was a big bird
And cows in a herd.

Rebecca Wilson (11)
Thomas Lord Audley & Language College

Imaginary Journey

I can see a man driving down a road,
All of a sudden he ran over a toad,
I saw a pub, inside sat Miss Jabb,
Downing a pint of beer,
Driving a bus, I saw a deer!
We shot down the highway,
Life begins at 14, my dad would say.

Liam Bingle (11)
Thomas Lord Audley & Language College

Rainforest

A tropical paradise, a temple of jungle,
A treetopped wonder, nature's playground,
An intricate world of renaissance and radiance.

An undiscovered marvel of superior scenery
An extraterrestial dream with incomprehensible texture,
A world emitting the signals of indistinct meaning.

A swirling, rippling pattern of the
Shrouded mysteries in a secret place.
A scenario of a fiery spark,
Merging with one of chilling gale.
Essence of an eternal rainbow,
Dancing in and out of a pool
Of voluptuous paradise.

Siôn Griffiths (11)
Westcliff High School For Boys

Maths Of Love

How do I add my love to you?
It multiplies when you say, 'I do'.
It subtracts when your heart says, 'no'.
It divides if you would tell me to go.

Graphs and equations show we're compatible
Your expressions tell me we're an ideal couple,
Loving you is prime factorisation.
What is the result of our algebraic equation?

Statistics will show us we're meant for each other,
We're like right angles we fit together,
We're a sequence that will go on forever,
Is there a solution for my endless love?

Shruti Kapoor (17)
Woodbridge High School

NEVER TELL A SECRET

Don't climb out the window tonight,
You wouldn't,
I might,
Please,
I look away, to the pictures on the wall.
You don't understand.
But I do! I want to scream.
I'm sick of bearing it.
I think of black creatures crawling over my sister's body,
Of white powder being bought and slipped into drinks.
Of boyfriends and windows and pictures on the wall.
I hear the sound of her leaving.
The branches swish.
Thud.
That's it, I think. She's gone.
It'll be your fault if she doesn't come back,
I can feel tears on my cheeks, the door opens.
Where's your sister?
Toilet.
It shuts again. Silence.
I look away from the window, to the pictures on the wall.

Rowena Knight (13)
Woodbridge High School